The Institute of Biology's
Studies in Biology no. 133

Ecological Evaluation
for Conservation

Ian F. Spellerberg
M.Sc., Ph.D., M.I.Biol.
Lecturer in Biology,
University of Southampton

Edward Arnold

First Published 1981
by Edward Arnold (Publishers) Limited
41 Bedford Square, London WC1 3DQ

ISBN 0-7131-2823-2

Photoset and printed by Photobooks (Bristol) Ltd

General Preface to the Series

Because it is no longer possible for one textbook to cover the whole field of biology while remaining sufficiently up to date, the Institute of Biology proposed this series so that teachers and students can learn about significant developments. The enthusiastic acceptance of 'Studies in Biology' shows that the books are providing authoritative views of biological topics.

The feature of the series include the attention given to methods, the selected list of books for further reading and, wherever possible, suggestions for practical work.

Readers' comments will be welcomed by the Education Officer of the Institute.

1981   Institute of Biology
                                      41 Queen's Gate
                                      London SW7 5HU

Preface

During the last ten years there has been a rapidly growing interest in the development of methods for determining conservation priorities. This interest has emerged from the ever increasing pressures on our natural environment, the growing number of extinct and endangered species, and the widespread loss of biotic communities. Although biological conservation is not a new subject, the ecological basis of conservation has been slow in emerging from the ideals and the philosophy of nature conservation. Only more recently have we seen some exciting developments in the application of ecology to the problems of evaluating species, natural areas and formulation of environmental impact assessment. The need for environmental education has never been greater yet at the same time the role of ecology in conservation and in planning so often receives scant attention.

This book has been written with frustration and with excitement. Frustration because it was inevitable that I could not discuss as many aspects and topics as I had wished. Excitement because much of what is called ecological evaluation is new, often controversial but nevertheless it is already contributing much to a better and more rational approach to conservation. The role of ecology in helping to decide conservation priorities for animals and plants and for natural areas is a major theme. The main objective is to describe as simply as possible the methods currently used in evaluation, to outline the ecological basis and to stimulate discussions on the application of the evaluation methods and so contribute towards environmental education.

I would like to acknowledge the inspiration provided by both students and colleagues and in particular I thank Barrie Goldsmith and Colin Tubbs for their constructive comments.

Southampton, 1981   I.F.S.

Contents

1 Biological Conservation and Evaluation

1.1 Some historical developments in biological conservation

An early and significant development in the emergence of biological conservation was the protection of large areas of land. For example in 1872 the Yellowstone National Park was established in North America, partly as a response to the considerable concern for protection of the environment from many kinds of pressures including the collecting of biological and geological specimens. Some of the world's first national parks were established in Australia, the first being the Royal National Park in 1886. Nearby in New Zealand the first National Park was established in 1894 and today it has ten National Parks which account for about eight per cent of the country's area.

The development of National Parks in Britain as a method of conservation had a slow beginning but in contrast to this the moves towards the protection and conservation of certain animal and plant groups were rapid. In 1889 a women-only group was formed with the aim of not wearing feathers of any bird not killed for the purpose of food (ostriches excepted) and it was from this that the now very large Royal Society for the Protection of Birds was formed. The National Trust for Places of Historic Interest and Natural Beauty was established in 1895 and this marked the commencement of protection of certain areas important for the biological and geological attributes. The Society for the Preservation of Wild Fauna of the Empire was established in 1903 and today it is the well known and successful Fauna Preservation Society. Rothschild in 1912 played a key role in the formation of the Society for the Promotion of Nature Conservation, and this group not only administers its own reserves but also coordinates the work of county naturalist trusts.

Today in Britain, as in many other countries, there is a bewildering array of societies, trusts, and other groups which all have a part to play in biological conservation. But perhaps the most notable development came in the field of legislation. For example one landmark was the National Parks and Access to the Countryside Act, 1949 which gave rise to a number of very important developments. The Nature Conservancy was created and their brief was to provide scientific advice on conservation and also to establish and manage reserves (which adequately represented major types of natural and semi-natural vegetation) with the organization and development of scientific services in this field. This Act led to the formation of the National Parks Commission which was to designate National Parks where there would be strict control of development.

This Act can be seen to be very appropriate on a very large scale but there was still a problem because there were many smaller areas of scientific interest that could not be established as national nature reserves. It was section 23 of this Act that was to go a step further and it gave the Conservancy a duty to notify planning authorities of any area which 'not being land for the time being managed as a nature reserve, is of special interest by reason of its flora, fauna, or geological or physiographical features'. These are what are called the Special Sites of Scientific Interest and they have been very important in the development of conservation in Britain.

There have been important changes since the time when the Nature Conservancy and the National Parks Commission was created in 1949. The Nature Conservancy is now the Nature Conservancy Council (with the Nature Conservancy Act, 1973 it became an independent statutory authority responsible to the Secretary of State for the Environment) and was divided off to leave the Institute of Terrestrial Ecology. The National Parks Commission has become the Countryside Commission. Further to this there have been a number of Acts which are aimed at the protection of named animals and plants (§ 2.4).

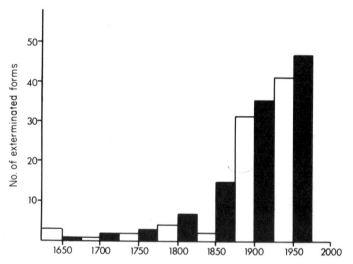

Fig. 1-1   The number of exterminated mammal forms (white bars) and bird forms (black bars) over the last three hundred years. Each bar represents a 50 year period. (From Ziswiler, J. (1967). *Extinct and Vanishing Animals.* Springer-Verlag, New York.)

To end this brief history we should note the beginning of developments on an international scale. It was UNESCO which was largely responsible for the formation of the International Union for the Conservation of Nature and Natural Resources (§ 2.1) which has made many achievements in the field of biological conservation. Equally successful has been the World Wildlife Fund which has played a very important role on the international scene. The Council of Europe's Information Centre for Nature Conservation was formed in 1967 and this was a very important international step which in 1970 led to the European Year for Nature Conservation. The Council of Europe has produced a series of short publications under the general title *Nature and Environment Series*. Topics include Aspects of forest management (No. 1), Soil conservation (No. 5), Evolution and conservation of hedgerow landscapes in Europe (No. 8), Threatened mammals in Europe (No. 10), and Heathlands of western Europe (No. 12).

In London on 5 March 1980 the World Conservation Strategy was launched and this sets out the objectives of resource conservation, the obstacles to achieving it, and the need for urgent action.

1.2 Aims of biological conservation

The case for biological conservation and the functions of wildlife (Table 8, p. 41) have been well documented. The rate at which species have become exterminated during the last 300 years has increased dramatically (Fig. 1–1). It is now believed that at least 25 000 plant species are threatened with extinction.

The rate at which biological communities have been destroyed in the last 200 years is equally dramatic. Over-grazing, de-afforestation and bad agricultural practices have all contributed towards diminished soil quality throughout vast areas of many countries. More than a third of the world's land surface is already desert or semi-desert.

The loss of biological communities arouses concern and the rate of loss is particularly alarming. One of the most remarkable landscapes of western Europe are the heathlands, and loss of lowland heathlands (Fig. 1–2 and 1–3) of southern England (and western Europe) is at a rate similar to that at which many

Fig. 1–2   Heathland in lowland Britain. Photograph by the author.

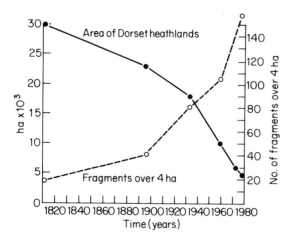

Fig. 1-3 The decline and fragmentation of Dorset (southern England) heathlands. (Data from Moore, N. W. (1962). *J. Ecol.*, **50**, 369–91, and Webb, N. R. and Haskins, L. E. (1980). *Biol. Conserv.*, **17**, 281–96.)

terrestrial and aquatic communities are being destroyed. The major factors contributing to the decline of heathlands include reclamation for agricultural purposes, re-afforestation and urbanization.

I suggest that the aims of biological conservation should therefore be (1) to safeguard a high level of richness of animal and plant species and (2) to manage wildlife resources wisely for the benefit and rational use by man. In some circumstances the preservation of a species of an area of land might be justified as part of the rational use of that natural resource.

1.3 Evaluation and ecological evaluation

Like 'landscape evaluation', 'ecological evaluation' now has common usage but its meaning is not often made clear. Although an evaluation may include value judgements, Fowler's *Modern English Usage* states that evaluate is a term of mathematics meaning to find a numerical expression for: hence, more generally, to express in terms of the known. It would seem reasonable to accept that an evaluation of a species, or a community, or a natural area could be based on ecology. The aims of an evaluation might be to determine the conservation requirements of a species, or it could be to assess the impact resulting from a change in land use.

Research in the Netherlands over the last ten years has resulted in identification of two types of ecological evaluation (PLOEG and VLIJM, 1978):

(1) Ecological evaluation as an assessment of ecosystem qualities *per se*, based on the thought that some ecosystem attributes are more important or interesting than others, regardless of their social interests.

(2) Ecological evaluation as a socio-economic procedure to estimate the functions of the natural environment for human society.

In simple terms, I like to think of ecological evaluation as a process involving the ecological assessment of an organism or environment. The application of ecological evaluation as introduced here can be explained by examining the topic at different levels as one might also examine ecology, for example at the species level, habitat level and community level.

Towards the end of the last century there were concerted efforts to preserve and protect certain groups of wildlife and also natural areas of land. We can be sure that the people who brought about these forms of early conservation were making an evaluation about their natural environment and as a result of this evaluation of the wildlife they could justify some form of protection of that wildlife. That is, a monetary value was not being suggested, they were not putting a price on the natural areas of land or on the groups of animals, they were assessing the status of the wildlife, finding out how many animals and plants of a certain kind there were, what the pressures on the wildlife were and then from this kind of information were proposing a form of conservation.

In a similar way we can today identify many animals and plants that are rare and endangered. The square-lipped or white rhinoceros (*Ceratotherium simum*), to name but one example of a mammal that is rare, has been the subject of much research and now rather than just saying it is rare we can, from studies of changes in its distribution and population, assess the status of this species and from an evaluation draw up proposals and plans in order to improve its status. One attempt to do this has come from the International Union for the Conservation of Nature (IUCN) in the form of the *Red Data Books* (§ 2.1). More recently there have been attempts to devise a combination of scientific and other methods of evaluation which help to elucidate the conservation needs or the degree of threat experienced by certain animal and plant species. The application of ecology in conservation and in the evaluation of a species' status is then sometimes supplemented with various other evaluation methods.

But conservation of a species might not always be the reason for evaluation. The opposite reason is also very important. Evaluation of a pest species' status (e.g. bracken, *Pteridium aquilinum*, in parts of Britain) needs to be undertaken before some form of control measures can be planned. Although not discussed here, the ecological evaluation of the status of pest species is a large and very important topic.

As important as the ecological evaluation of a species is the development of techniques and methods for the more complex habitat evaluation and priority ranking of natural areas. A hypothetical example illustrates in an elementary way reasons for the need to develop this relatively new aspect of biological conservation. A mining company has obtained permission to extract minerals underlying woodland and lowland heathland. The permission is such that the company may operate in two of the five available sites but not in all of the five sites. The decision as to which sites are to be mined now rests on the relative biological value of the different sites of woodland or heathland and ecologists have been asked to assess which of the two sites should be used. In this instance ecological evaluation would have important applications. This hypothetical example is but one area where ecological evaluation has and will be used more often in the future. In some parts of Britain, particularly in north-west England, there is a need for ecological evaluation particularly in connection with restoration of land and manipulation of derelict land containing industrial waste. In this context ecological evaluation has an important role in environmental impact assessment (Chapter 5). One important benefit of ecological evaluation could be improved communication. That is, the decision to conserve, manage or exploit wildlife resources is very often made not by the scientists but by the planner and the administrator. Economic, financial and other considerations have to be made before some course of action is recommended and ratified, and in order to form decisions the administrators and planners require results of research in a highly concise and quantitative form. Good ecological evaluation methods could be a basis for communication of ecological information.

2 Evaluation of Animal and Plant Species

Probably the most important and also the most common objective for the evaluation of a species is to propose some form of biological conservation. It could be conservation by active management, conservation of the species by providing protection in a nature reserve, conservation with protection by law, or it could be a combination of these and other aspects.

2.1 The Red Data Books

In 1934 an organization (L'Office International pour la Protection de la Nature) was founded which was later to evolve into the International Union for the Protection of Nature, and then in 1956 it became the International Union for the Conservation of Nature and Natural Resources. The IUCN, as it is now popularly known, has its headquarters in Morges, Switzerland and it works through a number of commissions, one of which is the Survival Service Commission. This Commission is concerned primarily with action to prevent the extinction of plant and animal species and also to preserve viable populations in their natural habitats. Since 1966 the Survival Service Commission has been collecting information on animal and plant species in order to help achieve these aims. The information is presented in synoptic form in volumes of the *Red Data Books* (Fig. 2–1). It was Sir Peter Scott who in the mid-1960s initiated these *Red Data Books*: each contains a long list of threatened species.

The task of gathering information for the production of these books is enormous and an evaluation or judgement first has to be made as to whether or not a species is to be entered in one of the volumes which include (1) Mammals, (2) Birds, (3) Amphibians and Reptiles, (4) Fish, (5) Angiosperms – flowering plants.

Until now, *Red Data Book* compilers were scattered around the world. This has now changed and the Species Conservation Monitoring Unit (SCMU) set up by IUCN's Survival Service Commission is now based at Cambridge, England. Members of the Survival Service Commission have in the past readily admitted that whether or not to include an animal and plant species has to be a matter of professional judgement. An example of part of a synoptic report is shown in Fig. 2–1. First the IUCN requires the common or popular name as well as the scientific name such as Galapagos giant tortoise (*Geochelone elephantopus*). The next relevant piece of information is the former and present distribution of the species, in this case the Galapagos archipelago. There are several races of this tortoise and 11 of the 15 original races were known to be present on the islands in 1974. In an evaluation of the status of a population it is necessary to have some knowledge of the numbers and also the method used to calculate the numbers.

SOUTH ALBEMARLE TORTOISE

Testudo elephantopus elephantopus   Harlan, 1827   (= T.e. vicina (Günther 1875))

Order   TESTUDINES   Family   TESTUDINIDAE

STATUS   Endangered.   Could well become extinct(7).

DISTRIBUTION   Cerro Azul, eastern Isabela (Albemarle), Galapagos, and
probably distributed through the whole southern end of Isabela.   At Iguana
Cove only one subspecies appears to be present, but near Vilamil one finds both
T.e. elephantopus and T.e. guentheri (1).   However, it may eventually be shown
that these two taxa should be combined, since Van Denburgh has found much
overlapping in morphological characteristics and apparent mixing.   Until 1925,
there was no barrier separating the two volcanos of southern Isabela and the
lava flow which occurred in that year still does not separate the tortoise
populations of Cerro Azul and Sierra Negra in a large sector along the
southern coast (7).

POPULATION   400-600 individuals (7), of which 276 were permanently marked by
January, 1974 (C.G. MacFarland, pers. comm.).   The population was somewhat
depleted by the activities of seamen in the past two centuries.   Extensive
slaughter in the late 1950s and late 1960s by employees of cattle companies
based at Iguana Cove, resulted in the virtual elimination of tortoises in this
area, leaving surviving populations still further to the east and west.
Poaching is still a problem in one area to the west, but the major threat at
present is predation by introduced mammals: to the west of Iguana Cove dogs
and cats destroy almost all the young and to the east, pigs destroy most nests
and dogs, cats and pigs kill the young.   Cattle and black rats are present
throughout the range of this subspecies (7).

HABITAT   In dry, transition, moist and grassy vegetation zones (2), originally
over most of the volcano (MacFarland pers. comm.).

BREEDING RATE IN WILD   Mating and nesting still occur normally, but there is
a great preponderence of adult animals, with few small or medium-sized
individuals to be found (7).

CONSERVATION MEASURES TAKEN   In 1959, Ecuador declared all uninhabited areas
in the Galapagos to be a National Park and made it illegal to capture or
remove many species from the islands, including tortoises or their eggs; in
1970, it became illegal to export any Galapagos tortoises from Ecuador,
regardless of whether they have been reared in captivity or the wild, and
whether from continental Ecuador or the islands; United States Public Law
91-135 (December 5, 1969) automatically prohibits importation of Galapagos
tortoises into the U.S.A., because their export from Ecuador has been declared
illegal (5).   A 1971 decree makes it illegal to damage, remove, alter or
disturb any organism, rock or other natural object in the Galapagos National
Park (7).   The Galapagos National Park Service wardens now visit the
Albemarle population frequently during the breeding/nesting season; in the
eastern area nests are protected with lava corrals and an attempt is being
made to control pigs by systematic hunting (8).   Lastly, since 1971, eggs have
been taken from wild nests to the Charles Darwin Research Station for hatching
and raising of young (MacFarland pers. comm.).

CONSERVATION MEASURES PROPOSED   Stationing of semi-permanent wardens in the
Western area to prevent poaching (6).

RDB-3.   IUCN © 1975   9(2)F   Code: 2.1.6.4.1.1 E

Fig. 2-1   An example of part of a synoptic report from the IUCN *Red Data Book* Vol 3.
This entry is for a Galapagos tortoise (*Geochelone* [*Testudo*] *elephantopus*).

Population sizes of the giant tortoise races have been calculated on the basis of numerous samples and extensive habitat surveys by researchers on the Islands (MacFARLAND *et al.*, 1974) and it has been found that most races number only a few hundred. Further to this, it has been possible to show from historical records that there has been a significant reduction in the size of the populations. Along with the population size estimates it is useful to have information on breeding rates in the wild and in this case it has been possible to examine the sex structure, size class structure and reproductive potential of the different races.

The habitat for the several races of the Galapagos giant tortoise is of course restricted to the Islands of the Galapagos archipelago and most suitable regions occur in limited transitional and moist grassy vegetation zones where in some cases there is competition from introduced mammals. This then identifies a further factor which has contributed towards the change in the tortoise populations. Of the 11 surviving races, eight are threatened with extinction by one of the following: decreased population size; predation on nests by introduced mammals; competition from introduced mammals. Human exploitation is now relatively unimportant, partly because Ecuador in 1959 declared all uninhabited areas in the Islands to be a National Park.

Having evaluated the current status of the Galapagos giant tortoise it is then possible to suggest and also implement conservation measures. Methods for the control of the feral mammals are being sought and in addition successful techniques have been found for the establishment of breeding colonies and the raising of young in captivity.

The *Red Data Books* are in themselves an invaluable source of biological information, providing a synopsis of the animal's or plant's status and also a brief account of the kind of conservation measures that should be or have been implemented. From the viewpoint of species evaluation there is a further important piece of information which is included (in each of the species accounts). This is the category of the species (Fig. 2–1). Each of the species is assigned to a particular category and these categories are defined in the following ways:

(i) *Endangered*   Taxa (that is species or subspecies) in danger of extinction and whose future survival is unlikely if the factors continue to operate. Included are taxa whose numbers have been reduced to a critical level or whose habitats have been so drastically reduced that they are thought to be in immediate danger of extinction.

(ii) *Vulnerable*   Taxa believed likely to move into the endangered category in the near future if the causal factors continue to operate. Included are taxa of which most or all the populations are decreasing because of over-exploitation, extensive destruction of the habitat or other environmental disturbance; taxa with populations that have been seriously depleted and whose ultimate security is not yet assured; and taxa with populations that are still abundant but are under threat from serious adverse factors throughout their range.

(iii) *Rare*   Taxa with small world populations that are not at present endangered or vulnerable, but are at risk. These taxa are usually localized within the restricted geographical areas of particular habitats or are thinly scattered over a more extensive range, for example, the Dorset heath (*Erica ciliaris*). This plant is abundant on heaths in the south of England but the species has declined dramatically as a result of the destruction and fragmentation of heathlands.

(iv) Out of danger   Taxa formerly included in one of the above categories, but which are now considered relatively secure because effective conservation measures have been taken or the previous threat to their survival has been removed. An interesting example of an animal in this category is the tuatara (*Sphenodon punctatus*), a lizard-like reptile which occurs on at least 30 islands around the coast of New Zealand. The conservation measures taken have included very strict protection for tuataras by the New Zealand Government and protective measures to prevent accidental entry of rats and cats to the islands on which this species is found.

(v) Indeterminate   Taxa that are suspected of belonging to one of the first three categories but for which insufficient information is currently available.

It might well be suggested that a certain amount of subjective judgement is used when a species is being considered for inclusion in one of the above categories. Is this subjective element undesirable? When the aims of the Red Data Books are considered as a whole then the subjective element in this evaluation is probably not very important. It is far more important to have available at least some kind of information, which after all helps to identify the relative conservation needs of the species. The nature of the conservation measures that are proposed may at times be disputed, but before that stage can be reached evaluation based on scientific studies should first be undertaken.

2.2   British Red Data Books

The first *British Red Data Book* (vascular plants) was published by the Society for the Promotion of Nature Conservation in 1977 (Perring and Farrell, 1977). Basic information required for the preparation of this book came from distribution maps which are available for Britain's plants and also for several groups of animals. These maps are prepared by the Biological Records Centre based in Huntingdon, England. This centre began in 1954 as the Distribution Maps Scheme of the Botanical Society of the British Isles and resulted in the publication of the Atlas of the British Flora in 1962. The Atlas contains distribution maps for each of the plant species using a system of dots in areas of 10 km^2 (Fig. 2–2).

Here then, at least for Britain's plant species, was information which could be used for an ecological evaluation of the species and for an assessment of their status. The species included in the first of the *British Red Data Books* are those recorded in 15 or fewer of the 10 km^2 from 1930 onwards. The final list contained 321 species and represents about 18% of the native or probably native flora. The next step was to provide information on the status of each of the 321 species and this was in fact a very extensive exercise for it meant the collection of ecological and other relevant information. The compilers of this *Red Data Book* were still not satisfied however and took the work of evaluation a step further by arranging the plant species in some order or priority and avoiding the subjective

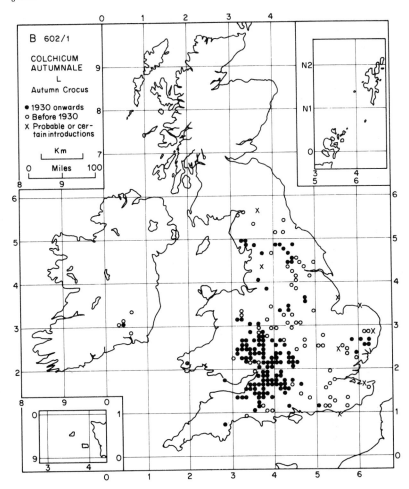

B 602/1

COLCHICUM
AUTUMNALE
L
Autumn Crocus

● 1930 onwards
○ Before 1930
X Probable or cer-
   tain introductions

Fig. 2–2 An entry from the *Atlas of the British Flora*. A symbol indicating the presence of a species in a 10 km. sq. of the Ordnance Survey National Grid is the basis of the scheme. (From Perring, F. H. and Walters, S. M. (1976). *Atlas of the British Flora*. E. P. Publishing Ltd.)

elements of 'rare' and 'endangered'. This exercise culminated in the calculation of a 'threat number' for each plant species: the method employed is particularly interesting (Table 1).

In the example taken from the *British Red Data Book* (Table 1), *columns 1 and 2* contain information about the distribution of the species but do not contribute to the threat number. *Column 3* refers to Great Britain and the first entry gives information about past and present distribution while the second entry contributes to the threat number based on the following: 0 = decline of less than 33%; 1 = decline of 33% to 66%; 2 = decline of over 66%.

Table 1   A table of threat numbers for British Plants. (From Perring, F. H. and Farrell, L. (1977). *Brtish Red Data Books*: **1** Vascular Plants. S.P.N.C.)

SPECIES	Ireland (H)	Channel Isles (S)	Great Britain (GB) I	Total I	Attractiveness I	Conservation I	Remoteness I	Accessibility I	Threat number	IUCN category
	1	2	3	4	5	6	7	8	9	10
Minuartia stricta	—	—	1/1	0	1	4	1	1	1	2	9	V
Muscari atlanticum	—	—	10/17	1	17	0	2	2	2	2	9	V
Narcissus obvallaris	—	—	7/9	0	7	2	2	1	2	2	9	R
Neotinea maculata	19/32	—	1/1	0	1	4	2	2	0	1	9	R
Oenothera stricta	—	4/4	10/29	2	12	1	2	1	1	2	9	R
Ophrys fuciflora	—	—	4/6	1	10	1	2	1	2	2	9	R
Paeonia mascula	—	—	1/2	1	1	4	2	0	0	2	9	V
Phyllodoce caerulea	—	—	3/3	0	4	3	2	1	1	2	9	V
Polygonatum verticillatum	—	—	4/10	1	5	3	2	1	1	1	9	V
Polygonum maritimum	1/1	1/3	2/11	2	2	4	0	2	0	1	9	E
Potentilla rupestris	—	—	3/3	0	3	3	2	2	1	1	9	V
Ranunculus ophioglossifolius	—	0/1	2/4	1	2	4	0	1	1	2	9	E
Rhinanthus serotinus	—	—	5/68	2	10	1	1	2	1	2	9	V
Selinum carvifolia	—	—	2/5	1	2	4	0	1	2	1	9	V
Senecio cambrensis	—	—	5/5	0	6	2	1	2	2	2	9	R
Taraxacum acutum	-	—	2/2	0	2	4	0	2	1	2	9	V
Taraxacum austrinum	1/1	1/2	1/2	1	2	4	0	1	1	2	9	V
Taraxacum glaucinum	—	—	2/4	1	2	4	0	1	1	2	9	V
Tetragonolobus maritimus	—	—	9/9	0	9	2	1	2	2	2	9	R
Trichomanes speciosum	22/47	—	8/15	1	8	2	2	2	1	1	9	V
Trifolium bocconei	—	1/1	2/3	1	5	3	1	1	1	2	9	R
Valerianella rimosa	9/41	—	9/96	2	10	1	0	2	2	2	9	V
Veronica verna	—	—	1/8	2	8	2	0	1	2	2	9	E
Woodsia ilvensis	-	—	4/12	2	4	3	2	1	0	1	9	V

Column 4 refers to Great Britain and the first entry gives the number of extant localities of the species known to the Biological Records Centre (in effect the number of 1 km^2 in which it has been recorded) and the second entry contributes to the threat number as follows: 0 = 16 or more localities; 1 = 10–15 or more; 2 = 6–9 localities; 3 = 3–5 localities; 4 = 1–2 localities.

Column 5 is an assessment of the attractiveness of the species (for collectors) and is recorded in the following way: 0 = not attractive; 1 = moderately attractive; 2 = highly attractive.

The conservation index is provided in *column 6* in the following manner: 0 = more than 66% of localities in nature reserves; 1 = between 33% and 66% of localities in nature reserves; 2 = less than 33% of localities in nature reserves; 3 = the same as 2 but is used where sites are subject to exceptional threat.

Columns 7 and 8 are subjective judgements of the relative ease with which the species can be reached by the public: 7 refers to the remoteness of the locality and 8 refers to the ease with which the species can be reached at the locality. In both cases 0 = not easily reached, 1 = moderately easily reached, 2 = easily reached.

Column 9 is the threat number and this is obtained by adding the values in columns 3 to 8; the maximum value that can be obtained is 15. *Column 10* is the IUCN *Red Data Book* category (§ 2.1).

The *British Red Data Book* is a rational attempt to evaluate plant species and to assess the relative conservation requirements of the species by assigning a threat number. Although it is tempting to be critical of the choice of categories used in the calculation of these threat numbers, there is much to be gained from a rational assessment of their usefulness. Undoubtedly there are many difficulties in selecting the categories and these do need discussion, but such an exercise can provide an insight into the problems of choosing the categories and also into the different conservation requirements of different kinds of animal and plant groups.

2.3 Evaluating species in natural areas

As a basis for discussion it is useful to consider one recent account (ADAMUS and CLOUGH, 1978) in which the authors reviewed species characteristics which could usefully be employed for evaluating whether or not a species is suitable for protection and indeed whether or not it should be considered. That is, these authors were attempting to define species characteristics which might assist in an evaluation of whether or not a species is suitable for protection in natural areas (Table 2). The first species characteristic was site tenacity and is the probability that a species will occur at the same general site or natural area for a specified period of years (a site being a place where a population occurs at some time in the life cycle of the species). An example of a species with a high breeding site tenacity is the gannet (*Sula bassana*) which has been known to nest on certain small islands for hundreds of years. Such islands could be designated as nature reserves for the protection of the gannet but in the case of other animals it might be useful to consider further aspects of the species' ecology. For example the feeding localities of some wading birds might also be usefully established as nature reserves although the birds do not use the areas as breeding sites.

Related to site tenacity is seasonal mobility, that is the tendency of a species to remain at the same general site and not migrate to other areas. Adamus and Clough believe that those species which usually have a limited mobility are more suitable for protection in nature reserves because a greater proportion of the habitat needs of the species can be protected in the reserve.

A rare orchid might be successful in a reserve of one hectare whereas a large herbivore species might require an area of many thousands of hectares. Spatial requirements are further complicated by the very characteristics of the area and by interspecific relationships, e.g. competition for an ecological resource. It is important therefore that all the ecological requirements be considered together with spatial requirements. A further and related characteristic when evaluating a species as suitable for protection in natural areas is the dispersion (spatial distribution) of the species. Two examples already mentioned illustrate the kinds of dispersion that can occur: large populations of gannets on small islands; the Dorset heath (*E. ciliaris*) which is found on the highly fragmented heathlands of southern England. The latter is a plant which might well deserve special protection because its pattern of distribution has reached a stage where there are now some isolated populations of this species. The gannet, although found in relatively small areas, does occur in large numbers and has considerably better powers of dispersal.

Table 2   Characteristics for evaluating species in natural areas (ADAMUS and CLOUGH, 1978).

Suitability	Desirability
Site tenacity	Relative scarcity
Seasonal mobility	Status changes
Area size needs	Endemicity
Spatial distribution	Peripherality
	Habitat specialization
	Habitat scarcity
	Susceptibility to immoderate human presence
	Other unusual or unique scientific values
	Aesthetic amenities and use

Adamus and Clough have listed a number of additional characteristics under the general heading of 'desirability'. This is meant to relate to those species which deserve or need special protection. The first of these is rarity or relative scarcity but as has been suggested above, we can think in terms of rarity in a number of ways. An excellent summary of the kinds of dispersion that characterize rare species has been given by DRURY (1974). As a definition of a rare species he suggests either a wide separation of small populations so that interbreeding between populations or sub-populations is seriously reduced or eliminated, or restriction to a single population. For example some of the large birds of prey occur in very small numbers but scattered widely over a large geographical area whereas some of the alpine plants occur in small numbers in few areas throughout their geographical distribution. Drury includes a third type of distribution which is characteristic of a rare species: even if the species occurs in large numbers it is restricted to a small number of localities.

Two further characteristics which have been mentioned (§ 2.2) and which are included by Adamus and Clough are the change in status of the species (decline in numbers or sites) and whether or not the species is endemic. Both of these are important when evaluating a species for protection but the next characteristic is perhaps even more interesting from the point of view of both genetics and ecology: some species occur as remnant populations or there may be populations that are peripheral to the main area of distribution. There are many plant and animal species in Britain which are at the northern limit of their geographical distribution and many of these may be of particular interest to those concerned with biological conservation. For example the sand lizard (*Lacerta agilis*), although known to occur throughout most of Europe, has a fragmented and restricted distribution in Britain. The scientific importance of what might be called a 'peripheral' species, could be added to the list of features when evaluating the species for protection in natural areas.

2.4 Legislation and evaluation of species

Some animal and plant species are protected by law and this protection is a form of conservation. Wildlife conservation law had its beginnings centuries ago in hunting and sport. The protection of wildlife for its own sake is a comparatively recent enterprise. In the United States legislation early this century was directed at protection of the American bison (*Bison bison*) and the bald eagle (*Halioectus leucocephalus*). Not until the 1960s was legislation in the United States specifically designed for endangered species.

In New Zealand, where there is a bewildering array of Acts concerned with conservation, the Animals Protection Act 1907 was the first legislation giving protection to native fauna. It was not until 1953, when the Wildlife Act appeared, that New Zealand had adequate legislation to protect wildlife.

The Antarctic regions have been at the centre of discussions on wildlife conservation law for many years. The Antarctic Treaty Act 1967 forbids those subject to British Law to kill, interfere with, molest, or take any native mammal or bird in the Antarctic.

In Britain the law relating to wildlife was directed at the avian fauna as far back as 1880, and today this has culminated in the Protection of Birds Act 1954–67. More recently badgers (*Meles meles*) have been the focus of attention and this mammal has been given protection by the Badgers Act 1973. Tree preservation orders and conservation area orders in town and countryside planning legislation provide some protection for trees, and legislation for specific plants came with the Conservation of Wild Creatures and Wild Plants Act 1975. A limited form of protection, by way of restricting killing and hunting in breeding seasons and at other times, applies to several groups of animals: for example the Deer Act 1963 and the Conservation of Seals Act 1970. A more recent act is the Endangered Species (import and export) Act 1976. This was the British response to Resolution Number 14 of the 7th General Assembly of the IUCN, which called upon all governments to restrict the importation of rare animals and to support the efforts of the countries of origin to preserve animals in danger of extinction. At the present time there are proposals for further wildlife and countryside legislation in Britain.

Regrettably in many countries, strictly scientific considerations can and indeed have been outweighed by historical and political considerations in the preparation of legislation. An example of this can be seen in the list of plant

Table 3   Schedule 2 of The Conservation of Wild Creatures and Wild Plants Act 1975. (HMSO, London). Categories from the IUCN Red Data Book (§ 2.1) and the threat numbers from the British Red Book (§ 2.2) have been added.

Species of protected plants

Threat No. and IUCN category	Common name	Scientific name
7V	Alpine Gentian	*Gentiana nivalis*
5R	Alpine Sow-thistle	*Cicerbita alpina*
7R	Alpine Woodsia	*Woodsia alpina*
9V	Blue Heath	*Phyllodoce caerulea*
10V	Cheddar Pink	*Dianthus gratianopolitanus*
10V	Diapensia	*Diapensia lapponica*
8V	Drooping Saxifrage	*Saxifraga cernua*
10V	Ghost Orchid	*Epipogium aphyllum*
9V	Killarney Fern	*Trichomanes speciosum*
12E	Lady's-slipper	*Cypripedium calceolus*
—	Mezereon	*Daphne mezereum*
11V	Military Orchid	*Orchis militaris*
11V	Monkey Orchid	*Orchis simia*
9V	Oblong Woodsia	*Woodsia ilvensis*
11V	Red Helleborine	*Cephalanthera rubra*
8V	Snowdon Lily	*Lloydia serotina*
11V	Spiked Speedwell	*Veronica spicata*
6R	Spring Gentian	*Gentiana verna*
9V	Teesdale Sandwort	*Minuartia stricta*
6R	Tufted Saxifrage	*Saxifraga cespitosa*
7R	Wild Gladiolus	*Gladiolus illyricus*

species included in Schedule Two of Britain's Conservation of Wild Creatures and Wild Plants Act 1975. This list of plant species (Table 3) does not contain all the species with high threat numbers: there are only a few species in this list with a threat number between 11 and 13 inclusive, but there are 46 species with a threat number of this value in the British Red Data Book. Obviously the criteria used in the selection of those species included in the Act are different from the criteria on which the threat numbers are based. This demonstrates the need for further research into evaluation methods.

Acts such as those mentioned above do provide interesting reading and it is illuminating to follow the arguments and discussions that have led to certain species being listed while others receive little mention. Despite the problems involved in selecting the species to include in such Acts, it is pleasing to find that in some Acts there is provision for a review of the Schedules every few years. With reference to the Conservation of Wild Creatures and Wild Plants Act 1975, the Nature Conservancy Council is required to review the schedules every five years and to 'advise the Secretary of State if any wild creature or plant has become so rare that its status is being endangered by any action designated as an offence under this Act and it should be included in Schedule 1 (animals) or 2 (plants) – or has become so common that its status is no longer endangered and it should be removed'. This Section of the Act should therefore provide an opportunity to improve the methods of evaluation when a species is being considered for protection by law.

2.5   The valuation of wildlife species

It has on occasions been suggested that monetary units be used for assessment of plant and animal species, habitats and biotic communities. This approach has been attempted in several countries and HELLIWELL (1973) had presented a case for assigning notional monetary values to wildlife resources in Britain. Helliwell's system for valuing individual wild species is based on factors such as abundance, conspicuousness and material value. Scores for each of these factors are multiplied together (e.g. *Calluna vulgaris* is about 320) and it is suggested that this be multiplied by 10 000 to give a 'shadow price'. The shadow price for a few species in Britain is shown in Table 4. Helliwell concluded that the total value for all species of animals and plants in Britain should be approximately 5–6000 million pounds.

The use of monetary units may have merit in some circumstances but it is important to recognize that the subjective elements in evaluation can not be avoided by the use of monetary units. It remains preferable to evaluate wildlife on the basis of ecological and biological principles.

Table 4   Suggested 'shadow prices' for representative species in Britain (HELLIWELL, 1973).

Quercus robur	£81 920 000
Salix caprea	£30 000 000
Fagus sylvatica	£21 480 000
Calluna vulgaris	£ 6 400 000
Acer pseudoplatanus	£ 3 200 000
Red deer	£ 2 000 000
Tilia cordata	£ 2 000 000
Galium saxatile	£ 640 000
Ptarmigan	£ 320 000
Polecat	£ 300 000
Primula farinosa	£ 80 000
Lloydia serotina	£ 20 000

3 Evaluation of Natural and Semi-natural Areas

The environment has many features which can usefully be evaluated by appropriate methods. For example just as it is possible to evaluate the landscape, buildings or villages it is also possible to make an ecological evaluation of natural and semi-natural areas. The aim here is to draw attention to the limited way in which ecology is currently used in the evaluation of the biotic and physical environment. The examples presented are terrestrial but they could equally well have been based on surveys and evaluations of marine and fresh-water communities.

Ecological evaluation of natural and semi-natural areas is a recent but poorly-defined subject and it is useful therefore to identify stages in the methods and also the scale of approach. There are at least two stages in evaluation: (1) a biological or ecological survey; (2) an evaluation of the wildlife, the habitats, and the biotic communities, based on selected criteria.

For more than a century, biologists have mapped the distribution of animals and plants and have prepared species lists. For an equally long period of time the inventories produced have been of use to international, national, and local organizations. Simple species lists and the classification of habitats have both contributed to the value of a biological survey. In turn, an evaluation has to be based on the collection of biological, ecological and other related data in both quantitative and qualitative forms.

The scale of the evaluation can be tremendously varied. That is, the limits within which the survey and the evaluation is conducted must be defined: the evaluation could be directed at a hedge, or it could be country-wide. The scale of the evaluation methods described here are such that they could be employed for areas ranging from less than a hectare to an area of several hundred hectares.

3.1 Surveys of biotic communities

In so much as there is an obvious requirement for an ecological basis for biological conservation, one prerequisite for evaluation of natural and semi-natural areas is a biological and ecological survey. An ecological classification of habitats has been extensively researched by the ecologist Charles Elton. A chart based on Elton's research and modified by the 'old' Nature Conservancy shows major terrestrial habitat types which could be found in a lowland area of England. The classification depends on four main categories, habitat systems (e.g. terrestrial, aquatic), formation types (e.g. open ground, scrub, woodland), vertical layers (e.g. ground, low canopy) and qualifiers (e.g. deciduous, conifer, mixed) as indicated in Fig. 3–1. The use of structural characteristics in classification of habitats has important applications when recording habitat

Chart of Animal Habitats (excluding aquatic habitats)

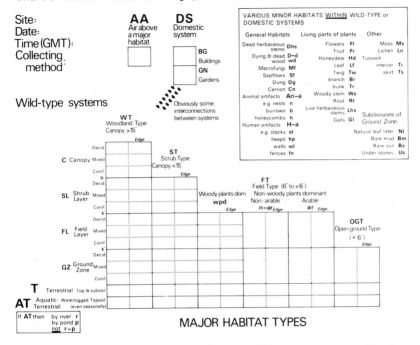

Fig. 3–1 A recording system of major habitat types. This system was prepared by the 'old' Nature Conservancy and is based on ELTON's (1966) classification of habitats. Appropriate information is scored in the boxes.

diversity and faunal diversity but of equal importance is a standardized procedure. An extensive and most useful method for ecological surveys was described by BUNCE and SHAW (1973) where the aim was to classify woodland ecosystems as a basis for their future conservation. For sampling purposes, a plot size of 200 m^2 was adopted as the basic unit and within this, four additional plot sizes provided a method for estimation of sample heterogeneity. All species of vascular plants and their percentage cover could be recorded on data sheets and so also could information on tree and shrub vegetation. Working from a plot size of 200 m^2, the habitat records were based on a careful selection of categories (Fig. 3–2). This procedure provides an account of diversity within a plot and it has been used in several national woodland surveys.

It is all too easy to design methods for biological surveys which are not based on precisely measured variables. The success of any evaluation method will depend very much on good sampling techniques and Bunce and Shaw in this instance have identified this requirement as well as identifying the need for precision. Their method which uses Elton and Miller's classification of habitats by structural characters (ELTON, 1966) goes a long way to achieving an ecological approach.

```
A  TREES - MANAGEMENT
   7 Cop. stool        8 Singled cop.      9 Rec. cut. cop.    10 Stump hard.n.w.
   11 Stump hard.old   12 Stump con.new    13 Stump con.old    14

B  TREES - REGENERATION
   15 Alder            16 Ash              17 Aspen            18 Beech
   19 Birch            20 Hawthorn         21 Hazel            22 Holly
   23 Hornbeam         24 Lime             25 Oak              26 Rowan
   27 Rhododendron     28 Sweet chestnut   29 Sycamore         30 Wych elm
   31 Other hrwd.      32 Scots pine       33 Yew              34 Other con.

C  TREES - DEAD (= HABITATS)
   35 Fallen brkn.     36 Fallen upstd.    37 Log. v.rotten    38 Fall.bnh.>10cm
   39 Hollow tree      40 Rot hole         41 Stump <10cm      42 Stump >10cm

D  TREES - EPIPHYTES AND LIANES
   43 Bryo.base        44 Bryo.trunk       45 Bryo.branch      46 Lichen trunk
   47 Lichen branch    48 Fern             49 Ivy              50 Macrofungi

E  HABITATS - ROCK
   51 Stone <5cm       52 Rocks 5-50cm     53 Boulders >50cm   54 Scree
   55 Rock outcp.<5m   56 Cliff >5m        57 Rock ledges      58 Bryo.covd.rock
   59 Gully            60 Rock piles       61 Exp.grav/sand    62 Exp.min.soil

F  HABITATS - AQUATIC
   63 Sml.pool <1m²    64 Pond 1-20m²      65 Pond/lake>20m²   66 Strm/riv. slow
   67 Strm/riv. fast   68 Aquatic veg.     69 Spring           70 Marsh/bog
   71 Dtch/drain dry   72 Dtch/drain wet   73                  74

G  HABITATS - OPEN
   75 Gld.5-12m        76 Gld. >12m        77 Rky.knoll<12m    78 Rky.knoll >12m
   79 Path <5m         80 Ride >5m         81 Track non-prep   82 Track metalled
```

Fig. 3–2 A recording scheme for habitats as suggested by Bunce and Shaw (1973), *J. Environ. Manag.*, **1**, 239–58.

Site data sheets have been designed for use in surveys and classification of marginal land in agriculture landscapes. They provide both an interesting comparison with the data sheets already mentioned and a reminder of the existence of semi-natural but important habitats. The datum recorded includes information of vegetation community structure, vegetation diversity and landscape quality.

Surveys directed at small semi-natural areas including hedgerows, (many of which have potentially important roles in wildlife conservation) are as equally important as large scale surveys (POLLARD *et al*, 1974).

The type of surveys described here could form a basis for the evaluation of biotic communities. In many evaluation methods there is a biological and or ecological survey incorporated in that evaluation. This is not to say that the survey has no value on its own. At one workshop on ecology and planning (HOLDGATE and WOODMAN, 1975) it was recognized that the basic ecological survey was one of four categories of advice provided by ecologists. It was agreed that the basic ecological survey should at least consist of a vegetation and land use survey, linked to topographical details. In addition it was thought important to identify zones of high ecological vulnerability to potential developments and that 'wild life evaluations' overlapped with 'vulnerability evaluations'.

The need for standardized descriptions for large scale biological surveys is particularly important. Much of the success and reliability of any ecological evaluation will depend on a rigorous approach to standardization. In this context the National Vegetation Classification of British vegetation types (based at The University of Lancaster) was launched in 1976. The plan is to produce a list and description of communities from natural, semi-natural and major artificial habitats. Probably the largest single body of systematically collected ecological information, these data are to be published in a two-volume manual some time after April 1982 (John Rodwell, pers. comm.).

3.2   Criteria used in evaluation of biotic communities

An outline of the methods employed in three schemes provides us with a representative sample of the criteria used in evaluations of natural and semi-natural areas. In 1974 TANS saw a need for an evaluation scheme of biotic natural areas in Wisconsin. He devised a scheme for priority ranking of natural areas based on the allocation of points, the more points awarded the higher the ranking. The criteria were divided into four categories (biological characteristics, physical characteristics, degree of threat, availability for protective ownership) and points assigned to separate criteria in each category. For example, in the first category, up to 10 points could be awarded for the quality of the main biological features, up to 6 points for the commonness of measure of importance of the natural area, and up to 5 points for community diversity. The quality would be measured by the richness of species, plant community structure

Table 5   Suggested features and feature categories to be considered in evaluating natural areas. (Gehlbach, 1975. *Biol. Conserv.*, **8**, 79–88).

Features and categories (numerical value)	Considerations
I **Heritage value** (1)	Presettlement landscape;
A Late seral stage (1)	either approximating the climax or in
B Climax condition (2)	virgin condition
II **Educational utility** (2)	Size sufficient for protection (includes buffer
A One special feature (1)	zones) or manipulation; history of study,
B Two special features (2)	present study, accessibility, demonstration
C Three or more special features (3)	value, etc
III **Species significance** (3)	Status in world, North America, and Texas,
A Peripheral species, hybrid zones (1)	in this order, for evaluating rarity and
B Rare, relict, or endemic species (2)	endangerment; Texas alone for evaluating
C Endangered species (3)	other categories
IV **Community representation** (4)	Diversity with attention to localised or relict
A Two or more community-types (1)	situations; geographic variants of a type,
B Community or dominance-types novel to preservation system (2)	and coverage of existing preservation system
C Localised or relict and novel types (3)	
V **Human impact** (5)	Degree of damage; nature of succession
A Possible but not imminent (1)	based on relative stress of physical
B imminent, *i.e.* planned (2)	environment; and suitability of restorative
C In progress but features salvageable through succession with management (3)	processes, either natural or cultural, if protection is afforded

and integrity and extent of human interference. For example, an area of highest biological quality would be an ideal community type with no disturbance (10 points) and in contrast 2 points might be awarded to a low quality area where human interference had resulted in the loss of biotic community structure. Guidelines for collection of quantitative data are not provided in detail, but nevertheless it should be noted that Tans' evaluation system is not designed to finalize an area's priority ranking: comparative ranking is the objective.

An evaluation scheme proposed by GEHLBACH (1975) for both professional and amateur use, provides a simple key for identification of plant community types, e.g. succulent desert, tall grass or deciduous woodlands then a standardized survey method on which to base evaluation and priority ranking. Using five features of the natural area. points are awarded in respect to the importance of these features for conservation (Table 5). Under each feature, categories of that feature are ranked and given values accordingly. A natural area score is obtained by multiplying each feature by its appropriate category value and adding the products. Gehlbach considered that it is least important whether the site is in or near a climax condition and that it is most critical to ascertain the extent and nature of human interference.

Obviously there is no better way to assess a scheme than to test it and a particularly useful way of obtaining constructive criticism is to arrange for students to test a scheme. The postgraduate Conservation Course at University College London has in the past provided many such opportunities and one particular evaluation scheme is well worth noting. A simple but quantitative and objective scheme proposed by GOLDSMITH (1975) was based on a case study and made use of a transect across three distinct land systems: un-enclosed upland, enclosed cultivated land, enclosed flat land. Habitats within each land system were identified as arable and ley, permanent pasture, rough grazing, woodland (deciduous/mixed, coniferous, scrub, orchards) hedges and hedgerows, and streams. The following parameters were determined for each habitat type: 1, Area (E); 2, rarity (R) for each habitat type calculated from R = 100 − % area per land system: 3, plant species richness (S) calculated from the number of flowering plant species in 400 m^2 plots; 4, animal species richness (V) considered to be correlated with stratification of the vegetation and so the number of vertical layers was recorded, as one (for grassland) to four (for well-developed woodland). An index of ecological value (IEV) for each kilometre square was determined as follows

$$IEV = \sum_{N}^{i=1} (E_i \times R_i \times S_i \times V_i)$$

These three evaluation schemes reflect the variation in approach of the many methods devised for evaluation of biotic communities. As would be expected they differ markedly in their relative use of ecology, biology, and value judgements. Nevertheless it is interesting to find that several criteria are common at all these schemes: ecological components feature most prominently in Goldsmith's method.

It comes as no surprise to find a subjective element in all three of the methods outlined. It should however be noted that the very selection of each of the criteria on which the evaluation is based, is in itself a subjective process. It is perhaps more important to consider whether or not these methods can be considered to be examples of ecological evaluation. Clearly there is in each of the methods an evaluation which is not based on ecology or not based on a precise measurement. In view of the fact that some criteria in all three methods (be it a rather simple measurement of animal species richness) does have a broad ecological basis, it seems reasonable to refer to them as examples of ecological evaluation.

Common to all three is that first important stage, the survey or inventory. The scale of each method can also be identified but what are the aims and how are the results of the evaluation to be used? Describing and identifying the comparative ecological value of the biotic communities seems to be the main aim although this is not clearly stated. The results of this kind of ecological evaluation could be used by planners, architects, and engineers along with the results from other evaluation procedures (e.g. assessment of agriculture potential, landscape evaluation). Undoubtedly the provision of ecological information in the early stages of planning is of paramount importance but it does not yet seem clear whether or not these methods provide the information required by, or expected by, planners (Chapter 5). Over the last few years there has been a series of meetings on the topic of ecology and planning but during the same time ecological evaluation methods have evolved. This being the case, there is ample opportunity for ecologists to discuss techniques of ecological evaluation with those who may be able to make use of the evaluation results. If ecological evaluation is to be applied, clear statements of the objectives are needed. Objectives of an ecological evaluation might be: (1) an evaluation of the conservation value of the wildlife at that time, (2) an evaluation to predict the effect or impact on wildlife resulting from change in land use; (3) evaluation to assess changes in the status of the wildlife resulting from recent impacts; (4) evaluation of natural areas for reserves.

An identical scheme for the evaluation of moorland, and for coastal communities and for an area with a large variety of communities would seem to be impracticable. A basic scheme which could be modified for different communities might however be useful so long as the methodology had been well researched.

3.3   Evaluation of woodlands

The widespread interest in woodlands has provided an impetus for the development of evaluation techniques. Whereas we could equally well consider alpine communities or river communities, the evaluation of woodlands is of particular interest simply because methods for ecological evaluation of woodlands have been well researched.

Although woodland was once the natural climax vegetation throughout most of Britain, it now covers less than ten per cent of the country and is predominantly in the form of woodland islands. The value of these woodlands in conservation is considerable and it is not surprising therefore that they have been the subject of much research. There are of course many types of woodlands in Britain and PETERKEN (1977) has drawn attention to the need to identify those types of woodland which are particularly important for habitat conservation. He has carefully identified five main woodland types which should have top priority for habitat conservation and these priorities are based on the concepts of past-naturalness and also non-recreatability. Briefly, the five British woodland types identified were as follows: relics of medieval wood-pasture systems; ancient high-forest woods; ancient coppice woods in which the coppice stratum has not obviously been planted; ancient woods on inaccessible sites; woods formed by a long period of natural structural development.

The ancient woodlands of Britain have been the particular concern of the Nature Conservancy Council. They have, for example, developed a method for recording and ranking the conservation value of ancient woodlands in southern England. It was first necessary to record on maps all the existing woods, particularly those which were thought to be of ancient origin. The grid references, area, structure and management of the woodlands was noted. A further stage involved a survey of the distribution of 110 woodland vascular plants as well as an assessment of the merits of some of the species as reliable indicators of ancient woodland. This was followed by a survey of many of the woods and data were obtained on the structure, stand type composition, and woodland vascular plant composition.

The evaluation of ancient woodlands for conservation could be determined on the basis of the plant and animal species richness and on the number of rare or protected species, or on some combination of the many criteria mentioned previously. Peterken has pointed out that such an approach would have two problems. Complete species lists of all groups of plants (and animals) would be difficult to obtain even for one wood. Complete species lists may also not be a good measure of woodland value because the inclusion of common and ubiquitous species (low value in terms of conservation requirements) could be misleading in the evaluation of the woodland.

Peterken's method is based on the use of indicator species and has been adopted by the Nature Conservancy Council for the ancient woodland survey. His assessment of the flora is relevant only to woodlands and is not affected by the typically grassland and other species that might be found on rides or on disturbed ground. Peterken's definition of a woodland species is defined as (*i*) species which can tolerate the shade of a closed woodland canopy, (*ii*) those which create the canopy, and (*iii*) others which in some way require woodland conditions. Eliminated from consideration in the evaluation are those species which become rapidly established in new woodlands. These species will be those which tend to disperse easily between woods or are abundant in varied habitats such as hedges and ditches. The woodland species remaining are those with poor colonizing ability, are found in long established woodland and are termed primary or ancient woodland species: e.g. *Aquilegia vulgaris* (columbine),

Campanula trachelium (bats-in-the-belfry), *Carex* spp. (sedges), *Lathyrus montanus* (bitter vetch), *Milium effusum* (wood millet), *Polystichum aculeatum* (hard shield-fern), *Oxalis acetosella* (wood-sorrel). A simple census of these woodland species seems to provide a good measure of ancient woodland floristic richness relevant to the woodland ecosystem.

Clearly the Nature Conservancy Council is aiming for an ecological basis for the evaluation of ancient woodlands. The major characteristics recorded at each wood include lists of critical indicator species: these being woodland vascular plants seldom found outside woodland, or indicators of long continuity, or in at least part of the region act as indicators of ancient woodland. The stand types (PETERKEN, 1977) are recorded and also the structural forms of the tree and shrub species (e.g. standard tree in a coppice, a seedling) and species abundance is recorded on a 1–4 scale. Additional information included as in other surveys and evaluations of this type include the presence of conifer plantations, planted aliens, rides, paths, rivers, streams, banks, soil types, sites of special scientific interest or other designations.

The intensive and continual evaluation of Britain's ancient woods will undoubtedly be important for two main reasons: obviously the results will be used to assess the conservation value of the sites, secondly the research is doing much to develop methods for ecological evaluation. An extension of this work to other communities could improve and add much to the foundation of biological conservation.

3.4 Evaluation of forest resources

It has not been unusual for old established woodlands to be cleared and be replaced by exotic species as part of a programme of intensive afforestation. In eastern areas of Australia, vast areas of native eucalypt forest have been cleared and replaced by conifers as part of the intensive re-afforestation programme for the timber and woodchip industries. As the exploitation of these forests has grown to immense proportions, so also has the concern for the rapidly disappearing native resource. In one major publication of 1974 entitled *The Fight for the Forests*, ROUTLEY and ROUTLEY set about to make a careful and detailed assessment of this take-over of the Australian forests for intensive forestry. They logically ask whether or not forestry can be justified in purely commercial terms and linked to this they try to answer the question, is it relatively simple to predict consumption and how realistic are the predictions? But of far more importance and in reference to conversion of native eucalypt to radiata pine forests, is it possible to estimate the costs and benefits. This was a very important step for these authors and not only did they make a detailed cost benefit analysis they also attempted to put values on or make an evaluation of all aspects of the forests (Table 6). Theirs is a very exhaustive analysis but very briefly the factors considered are as follows and in terms of annuity values of dollars per acre.

(1) *Timber production*   Land values are costed at zero and this excludes administrative overheads which if added would increase the cost.

Table 6 Example of a proposed cost-benefit analysis of conversion of eucalypt plantations to radiata pine plantations, in terms of annuity values measured in dollars per acre. Direct components discounted at 5.5% over two rotations of 40 years each, and indirect components illustrated, with social discount rate of 3%. (Suggested by ROUTLEY and ROUTLEY, 1974.)

	Costs				Benefits			
Item	EL	PL	EH	PH	EL	PL	EH	PH
Direct market components								
(1) Timber production	1	8	4	8	1	7	3	9
(2) International trade (balance of payments, costs of protectionism, etc.)	0	2	1	3	0	1	2	3
Indirect components								
(3) Watershed values	1	1	1	2	3	2	4	2
(4) Wildlife and flora values	0	4	0	4	6	0	7	0
(5) Sustainability values	1	8	2	6	2	0	2	0
(6) Recreation (tourism, etc.)	2	2	1	1	4	4	2	2
(7) rural employment de-centralization, etc.)	0	0	0	1	0	2	1	4
Totals	5	25	9	25	16	16	21	20

Evaluations	EL	PL	EH	PH
Benefits less costs	11	−9	12	−5
Benefit/costs ratio	$^{16}/_5$	$^{16}/_{25}$	$^{21}/_9$	$^{20}/_{25}$

EL, Eucalypt on low-quality site, 100 miles from capital city.
PL, Radiata on low-quality site, 100 miles from capital city.
EH, Eucalypt on high-quality site, 300 miles from capital city.
PH, Radiata on high-quality site, 300 miles from capital city.

(2) *Investment and trade* It is considered that in Australia water is a scarce and more important resource than timber. In the watershed areas the conversion would result initially in disadvantages of erosion (Fig. 3–3) and it is not clear what effect pines have on run-off.

(3) *Wildlife, flora, landscape and diversity* The preservation of these is considered to be an enhancement and so therefore a benefit, their elimination as a cost. The criterion used is based on a comparison with other practicable forms of land use. Thus pine plantations are assigned a high cost for the elimination of these features and no benefit because there are few forms of land use for the initially rich areas in question which would do more to eliminate these features and which would preserve less. In contrast pine planted on already cleared land would have no cost in terms of these features and perhaps a small benefit. The

Fig. 3-3 This was once a eucalypt forest and it has been cleared as part of a woodchip project. (Photograph by John Turnbull.)

values here are likely to become more significant as natural areas disappear. That is, the Routleys believe that values will increase with scarcity and so therefore even more reason for the evaluation of the forestry programme.

(4) *Sustainability* This includes features affecting sustained yield over a long term such as characteristics of the soil. The authors feel that there may be a case for giving this feature a greater weighting because it will affect all the benefits of the pine plantation.

(5) *Recreation* Sites near cities are given higher values than those sites more distant from cities. There is some argument as to whether or not pine plantations are preferred to broadleaf forests for recreation.

(6) *Rural employment and decentralization* This is a very contentious issue and little emphasis is placed on this feature by these authors.

This cost benefit analysis is a major contribution to the evaluation of major impacts. It provides a model on which to base cost benefit analysis, both in Australia and in other countries.

3.5 Evaluation of physical features

The main theme of this book is the evaluation of biological resources with particular reference to ecological evaluation of biotic communities. The terrestrial environment has features other than biological: e.g. there are many locations which have scientifically important fossil deposits and there is very often a good case for their conservation. Indeed, our National Nature Reserves and other protected areas are not there just for the biological communities, and often considerable effort is made to protect geological, geographical and other physical features.

One particularly interesting physical resource which has been the subject of ecological evaluation is the area of limestone pavement found in Britain. The most extensive pavement areas or bare expanses of limestone occur on thick, massively bedded limestones of the lower carboniferous. Fissures and cracks in these pavements support a highly interesting flora and so an evaluation scheme for the conservation of the limestone pavements was based on the characteristics of this flora (WARD and EVANS, 1976). Pavements were compared using an index in two forms: (1) a floristic index which provides a means of comparing individual limestone pavements; (2) a compound floristic index which provides a basis for the comparison of groups of limestone pavements.

The floristic index (FI) was based on species abundance (a) ratings where $1 =$ one or two individuals and extremely sparse, $2 =$ locally abundant or widely scattered over the whole pavement but not abundant and $3 =$ abundant. There is also a weighting according to the allocation of the species to one of the following groups: nationally rare species; nationally uncommon species, or with marked regional distribution; nationally common species. Thus in the following formula

$$FI = 3\Sigma a_A + 2\Sigma a_B + \Sigma a_C$$

the A, B, and C species are weighted in the ratio 3:2:1 with a nationally rare species three times the value of a common species.

The compound floristic index (CFI) was based on the average abundance of each species occurring in a pavement group, re-scaled so that each species now ranges between 0–10 instead of 0–3, the formula provided by Ward and Evans is as follows

$$CFI = 3\Sigma c_A + 2\Sigma c_B + \Sigma c_C$$

where $c =$ average re-scaled abundance.

It is important to emphasize, as do the authors of this evaluation scheme, that the indices should only be regarded as guides to limestone pavement value, and not be taken as definitive values.

4 Site Selection and Design of Nature Reserves

4.1 Reserves for wild life

The setting aside of land for the protection of animals and plants is not new. For centuries tracts of land have been set aside for hunting and such areas managed and administered as they were provided sanctuaries for many forms of wildlife. The historically famous New Forest in England now 900 years old and once a Royal Forest has in the past, and is today, and important refuge for many rare animal and plant species: its richness in wildlife is often overlooked.

Throughout the world there is now an exciting array of reserves ranging from a few square metres of land to vast national parks and ocean sanctuaries. Single large trees (e.g. the ancient thorn-tree, *Crataegus monogyna*, at Hethel in Norfolk on the east coast of England) have been provided protection in small nature reserves. At the other extreme, large areas have been established as national parks in many continents; an ocean sanctuary has been established near Hawaii for hump back whales, *Megaptera novaengliae*, and the Antarctic continent contains many reserves for the protection of a wide variety of oceanic and terrestrial life.

We should also note that sanctuaries for wildlife are sometimes created in more indirect ways such as by virtue of National Trust Properties, preservation orders, and also by land set aside for the Ministry of Defence where a rich diversity of wildlife can often flourish, be it in an army firing range.

The selection and creation of a nature reserve can be achieved in a variety of ways, but nevertheless it usually commences with a biological survey followed by an evaluation of the biotic and geophysical components. Voluntary conservation organizations have, throughout the world, probably been the most important agents in these surveys and subsequently the selection and acquisition of nature reserves. In Britain, the Nature Conservancy Council is one body which has a responsibility for the selection, acquisition and protection of National Nature Reserves. This body, like others before it, have surveyed and reviewed the natural environment and have established criteria (site characteristics) on which to base the selection of nature reserves: some of these criteria are based on ecological concepts, some are biological and most are value judgements.

4.2 Criteria used in site selection

In Britain, possibly the most important and recent contribution to the conservation literature came in 1977 when *A Nature Conservation Review* was published (RATCLIFFE, 1977). In the two large volumes there is an extensive and comprehensive account of many key sites of importance to biological conservation in Britain. The objective of the review was, 'select according to established criteria of nature conservation value a series of sites which gives acceptable representation of all the more important features within the range of variation in natural and semi-natural ecosystems in Britain'. The process of site selection involves three basic stages: recording the intrinsic site features; assessing comparative site quality, choosing the national series of key sites. The following ten criteria used for site assessment and selection of reserves are discussed at length in the Review: size, diversity, naturalness, rarity, fragility, typicalness, recorded history, position in an ecological/geographical unit, potential value, intrinsic appeal. These and other criteria also feature in a number of other schemes designed with the specific objective of the ecological evaluation and the general assessment of sites for nature reserves. In so far as the acquisition of a nature reserve can be a specific objective in an ecological evaluation, it is valuable to consider some of these criteria in detail, despite the fact that different reserves are selected for, and have different functions. Geophysical aspects, although equally important, are not discussed here.

4.2.1 Area

It might seem reasonable to assume that the larger the area of a potential nature reserve, the greater value. It would seem more rational however that we ask, what is the reserve for, and to what extent does the area serve the specific requirements of the wildlife that we are trying to conserve? Even then however, some might still claim that the larger the area, the better for conservation, and often this is done in the belief that larger areas will support a greater number of species.

If we were to estimate the number of terrestrial snail species in an area of 0.2 hectares, then sample again over a larger area, and then again over a larger area

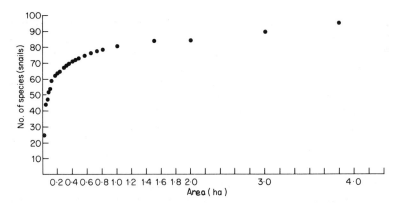

Fig. 4–1 A hypothetical species-area curve for non-marine mollusca of the British Isles. (Data from Kerney, M. P. (1976). *Atlas of the Non-marine Mollusca of the British Isles*, I.T.E. Cambridge. For method see § A.2.)

until we had samples from 24 areas, we could plot the relationship between number of species and area as in Fig. 4–1. It comes as no surprise to find that at first, the number of species increases with the size of the area being sampled, but as the area increases, the rate at which new species are added starts to diminish. In other words we could predict that there would be a certain area above which few new species are sampled.

Is it possible to show that this hypothetical species–area curve exists in nature? Results from many field studies have indeed shown that this particular species-area curve is real, and much of the evidence has come from studies on birds. In a recent report of research on number of bird species in British woods MOORE and HOOPER (1975) concluded that a ten fold increase in area virtually doubles the number of bird species in a fashion similarly to the MacARTHUR and WILSON island model (1967):

$$\log S = K \log A + \log C$$

where S is the number of species, A is the area, C is the number of species per unit area and K is a constant or it may be regarded as a measure of the degree of isolation of real islands.

We have been thinking of woodland area instead of simply saying area, and so therefore we are beginning to identify an ecological basis for this first criterion. That is, we have recognized one characteristic of the area; it is composed of a woodland community but can we classify the woodland and is the area covered uniformly? Despite the empirical relationship between bird species richness and area of wood, we would expect to find some woods which had either a lower or higher number of species than might be predicted from the species area curve. Geographical isolation for example might be a factor contributing towards a lower species richness. Another factor might be plant species composition. However, in deciduous forest plots of eastern United States a poor relationship has been found between bird species diversity and plant species composition, whereas a good relationship exists between bird species diversity and foliage height diversity (Fig. 4–2, also appendix A.2). This observation could usefully form the basis of a discussion on the optimum area for nature reserves.

When evaluating an area for the conservation of a particular taxon, those aspects already mentioned might usefully be considered. That is, sometimes an area is evaluated for the conservation of a rare or endangered species and then the question often asked is, what is the minimum area necessary for the survival of that named species? Some of my research on the ecology of reptiles provides an illustration of this approach and the information required to answer the question. In addition, the ecological basis of area as a criterion for the selection of reserves is expanded.

One objective of this reptile research has been to try and identify the minimum area required to support a viable population of sand lizards (*Lacerta agilis*). What are the ecological requirements of individual lizards and what are the ecological requirements of a population? At the individual level, it was possible, to determine the mean home range area of sand lizards in different study areas;

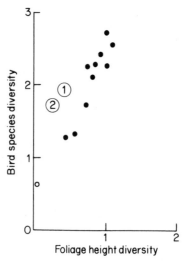

Fig. 4–2 A plot of bird species diversity against foliage height diversity of deciduous forest. (MacARTHUR and MacARTHUR. (1961). *Ecology*, **42**, 594–8. See § A.3 for method of determining foliage height diversity. Point 1 is census of tropical savannah and point 2 is census of pure spruce forest.)

this varied between about 480 m² and 1900 m². The home ranges overlap at each study area and there is variation in the mean area between study areas. Why is there a variation in mean home range size between sites? It is variable, probably because there is a difference in biotic and physical structures. At this stage, we begin to see that the answer to the question 'what is the minimum area for this species?' will depend very much on what the area contains and how the features satisfy the ecological requirements of the species.

The evaluation of a site cannot be based on area alone because in due course consideration has to be given to the cost of acquisition and also to the future management of the reserve. It does seem however that it is possible to qualify and quantify area or extent of the site particularly with reference to the requirements of the wildlife we are attempting to conserve. A particularly useful exercise is to consider whether or not the Nature Conservancy Council (with its limited budget) should aim to acquire large reserves or a series of small reserves (§ A.2).

4.2.2 Diversity

Poorly-defined criteria tend to diminish the usefulness of ecological evaluation. The use of area as a criterion is intelligible but diversity and richness are terms which need careful qualification. Diversity in the environment can be examined at different levels, commencing with a very broad approach and then continuing along a scale of increasing detail.

A simple approach is often expedient and so therefore we might first record the number and extent of plant communities in the area under consideration. Examples of plant communities include lowland dry heath, oak wood and reed swamp. We could therefore define diversity simply as the number of plant communities in the area.

An appropriate next level of investigation would be a measure of habitat diversity. Obviously there is a need to define and be able to quantify what we mean by a habitat. If we turn back to section 3.1 we see that there are ecological methods for classifying and quantifying habitats. Terrestrial habitats defined in this way could include carrion, dead wood, arable land, a hedge, or a wood. Elton's system of classification would include habitat systems subdivided into formation types and qualified by stratification into vertical layers (Fig. 3–1). A simple measure of habitat diversity would be the total number of habitats in a defined area.

When comparing areas and their relative value in terms of conservation, an area with a high diversity of communities or habitats would seem to be more valuable than an area with low diversity. In general this may be true but in some circumstances there may be a specific objective.

For example, if conservation of a xerophytic heath biotope is the objective then a uniform area or a poor diversity of plant communities would be acceptable, but if the conservation of a rich variety of insect fauna is the main objective then an area embracing several plant communities might be a better alternative.

We should not forget the successional processes or development of vegetation and so therefore for some areas it may be best to manage a sere or a seral community and not a climax community.

4.2.3   Species richness and species diversity

When evaluating areas for nature reserves, there may not only be a need to describe the ecological characteristics of the area, but also a need to compare areas. One possible method for the comparison of areas or habitats within one area is a measure of species richness or species diversity.

A simple count of the number of species is an indication of the species richness and in practice this is often restricted to a particular taxon or a group of organisms such as birds, aquatic arthropods or grasses. An alternative approach, and one which provides a useful measure of botanical variety, is to consider the variation in plant life forms (§ A.3).

Comparison of areas using species richness can be misleading because the total number of species recorded depends partly on sampling methods, sample size, and on the distribution patterns of the organisms. In order to overcome these difficulties a number of methods have been proposed for the measurement of species diversity, based on both the number of species recorded and on the number of individuals in the sample culminating in a diversity index.

There are many methods for the estimation of species diversity: the simplest is a count of the number of species (species richness) but this has several disadvantages (§ 4.2.1). The simplest index is the number of species divided by the total number of individuals in the sample. This index is strongly dependent on sample size but the sample size effect could be reduced by using the log of N:

$$D = \frac{S - 1}{\log N}$$

where D = index of diversity, S = number of species and N = total number of individuals.

The sequential comparison index (CAIRNS *et al.*, 1968) provides a useful index of relative differences in biological diversity. Following sampling in the area being considered, the organisms are collected together and arranged in a random fashion and are classified as being either different or the same as the preceding organism. For example in a sample containing four species the sequence might be:

```
 C  C  A  A  B  A  A  A  C  B  C  A  A  D  B  C  A  D  A  A  D  D  C  B  A
 1     2     3  4        5  6  7  8     9  10 11 12 13 14    15       16 17 18
```

and the index of species diversity $= \dfrac{18}{25} = 0.72$

Simpson's index provides a good index of species diversity although it gives relatively little weight to rare species:

$$D = 1 - \sum_{i=1}^{s} (p_i)^2$$

where D is an index of diversity, p_i is the proportion of individuals of species i in the community. For example in a sample with three species represented by 80, 15 and 5 individuals,

$$D = 1 - [(0.80)^2 + (0.15)^2 + (0.05)^2]$$
$$= 0.335$$

It should be appreciated that the calculations and interpretation of most indices of species diversity are not easy, that they all have their limitations and their biological meaning has been questioned.

As it is possible to define what is meant by species diversity, one of several indices could successfully be adopted for use in comparing areas. This can be done despite the underlying difficulties of describing the relationship between numbers of individuals and the number of species in a particular habitat, and whether or not trophic levels should provide the framework for an examination of species diversity. Much has been written about what is meant by diversity, the reasons for differences in diversity and there has often been a fissiparous tendency towards linking stability of ecosystems with species diversity. These problems should not however deter those who are concerned with conservation, from attempting to establish a factual statement about species richness or species diversity.

4.2.4 Rarity

Some ecological aspects of rarity have already been discussed (§ 2.3) but again it is important to emphasize that this criterion should be qualified. At what level is the species rare: local, regional, national, or at a zoogeographical level? Normally this aspect should be taken into consideration when using the presence of rare species for ecological evaluation. It is useful for example, to distinguish between (a) the relative number of that species in the study area, and (b) the number of 10 km² in which that species has been recorded in the *Atlas of British Flora.*

It is equally important to know the reasons for the rare status of the animal or plant because some species have a life style which is dependent on other species (not only for food) or on certain anthropogenic activities. For example the large blue butterfly (*Maculinea arion*) in Britain (Schedule 1, Conservation of Wild Creatures and Wild Plants Act 1975) has a very unusual life cycle involving wild thyme (*Thymus* sp.) and myrmica ants. It is probable that the complex life history contributed to the recent extinction of this butterfly in Britain. Some groups of plants are now threatened mainly as a result of changes in agricultural practices. We have in Britain today few good examples of water meadows and as a result of this, some water meadow plant species are very rare. Without knowing the cause then we cannot hope to take appropriate conservation measures and it is equally certain that if rarity is to be used as a criterion then we need to know much about the ecology of the rare organism.

4.2.5 Vulnerability

In an ecological sense, natural and semi-natural areas are not static but are continually changing. It is sometimes thought that once an area is declared as a reserve then it will be safe from any further interference or changes in land use and that the structure and components of both the animal and plant communities will remain unchanged. Plant and animal communities are dynamic: the patterns of abundance and distribution will change in space and in time. Natural changes such as succession can to some extent be managed or directed if indeed the objective is to preserve the existing nature of the plant and animal communities. Changes in water table levels have been known to cause drastic alterations to the fauna and flora of reserves.

There is no doubt that some nature reserves are vulnerable in the sense that their value as a reserve can be reduced by natural changes and also by other aspects such as nearby changes in land use or by the accidental introduction of new species. The vulnerability of an area could perhaps be considered in two ways. Some plant communities are vulnerable to certain types of impact, e.g. heathland is easily damaged by trampling. In another sense an area can be vulnerable simply by nature of its location e.g. alteration in land use such as the creation of industry in the surrounding areas could easily reduce the value of the area as a reserve. When evaluating an area for a nature reserve it is important to take into consideration the vulnerability of the area: it should be considered from the point of view of future management and from the point of view of potential changes to the adjacent areas. An ecological basis for vulnerability can readily be identified and the impact can be quantified.

4.2.6 Educational and scientific value

Natural or semi-natural areas will always have an important role to play as outdoor museums or as laboratories. Many reserves are managed in such a way as to provide a facility for education despite criticisms that once an area has been made a reserve there is no access for the public. The value of reserves for education and for scientific research is of paramount importance but it is difficult to measure and it is difficult to incorporate an ecological basis. Can this criterion be used satisfactorily in the evaluation of sites for nature reserves? An estimate of the value for educational purposes could be based on the extent to which the area is used for teaching ecology. In 1979 BOOTH and SINKER discussed the teaching of ecology in schools and suggested criteria for choosing sites for ecological field work.

4.2.7 Management

It is obviously important to consider the financial and administrative implications of maintaining the area as a nature reserve. Ecological characteristics of the area will partly determine the kind of reserve management and so

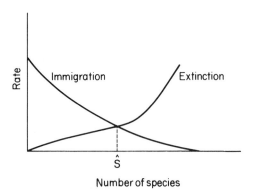

Fig. 4-3 A simplified representation of the equilibrium number of species (Ŝ) for an island. As the species present on the island increases, fewer of the immigrants are new so the immigration rate falls. As the number of species increases, the rate of extinction increases. Ŝ is where the curves intersect. (From MacArthur, R. H. (1972). *Geographical Ecology*. Harper and Row, New York and London.)

therefore there is every justification for considering this aspect along with the other criteria.

Inevitably the question has to be asked, what is the cost to maintain the area as a nature reserve. Obviously the budget will vary from reserve to reserve but nevertheless it is important and realistic to include this aspect in the evaluation. In 1976 the Nature Conservancy Council commissioned the post-graduate course in conservation at University College London to research management planning for National Nature Reserves. Several 'Conservation Reports' from that Course deal with this particular aspect.

4.3 Islands and ecological islands

A wood surrounded by agricultural land or an area of chalk grassland surrounded by roads and buildings is an ecological island. Wherever there is heterogeneity in the landscape and amongst plant communities, boundaries or zones will occur. For some organisms these zones will be suitable corridors for dispersal while for others the zones will act as barriers preventing dispersal.

The concept of nature reserves as ecological islands is both fascinating and valuable. It appears that some of the basic ecological principles which apply to real islands can usefully be applied to nature reserves in two ways: the reserve as a whole and the reserve structure of design and shape.

The composition and number of species on an island is basically the result of two processes, immigration of species and extinction of species. For a hypo-thetical island the equilibrium number of species ($\hat{S}$) is reached when immigration balances extinction. An over-simplification of this process is shown in Fig. 4–3 and MacArthur notes that this should be considered not as single sharp curves but as broad blurs, with a large area of intersection. This is because the curves can be considered to be averages of separate curves for different orders of arrival and extinction.

It is important to recognize that MacARTHUR and WILSON's model (1967) represents the number of species on an island as a dynamic equilibrium and therefore implies that when equilibrium has been reached, the species composition will continue to change. For a few years, the number of species might remain relatively constant but obviously this number will be dependant on the stability of both the ecological island and its environs. Factors which could increase or decrease $\hat{S}$ include the stability of the island environment, island size, remoteness and species richness of the source of colonization.

Factors which tend to change the equilibrium number of species are many and so also are the factors which will determine the type of species reaching the island reserve. The perimeter or boundary characteristics of the reserve will in part determine the species composition of the island nature reserve, as also will the species ability to disperse and overcome barriers. For example roads are, for some species, a barrier and OXLEY et al. (1974) suggested that divided highways with clearances of 90 m or more may be effective barriers to the dispersal of small forest mammals as bodies of water twice as wide.

The edge or boundary of an ecological island could support organisms not found elsewhere on the reserve. A transition zone between plant communities (ecotones) a habitat for many organisms (edge species). When considering the relationships between area and species richness, there could well be an interesting departure from the island model. This is because smaller areas will have, in proportion, a larger boundary zone. Therefore in a small reserve rather than the total number of species being small, there might be for some taxa an abundance of edge species which will contribute to a larger than expected total number of species. That is, small reserves could support a greater species diversity for a particular taxon than a slightly larger reserve simply because of the increase in those species whose ecology is supported by the boundary zone.

Table 7   Forest birds extirpated from Barro Colorado Island. (From Wilson, E. O. and Willis, E. O. (1975). In Cody, M. and Diamond, J. M. *Ecology and Evolution of Communities*. Belknap Press, Harvard.)

Species	Large for guild	Ground nester	Ground forager	Low density in tall forests	Immigration
Harpy eagle (*Harpia harpyja*)	++			a	f
Barred forest-falcon (*Micrastur ruficollis*)*	+			b	
Red-throated caracara (*Daptrius americanus*)*	+			c	f
Great curassow (*Crax rubra*)	++		+	a	e
Marbled wood-quail (*Odontophorus gujanensis*)	+	+	+	b	e
Rufous-vented ground-cuckoo (*Neomorphus geoffroyi*)	++		+	a	e
Barred woodcreeper (*Dendrocolaptes certhia*)*	+		+	b	e
Buff-throated Automolus (*Automolus ochrolaemus*)	+	+		b	e
Black-faced antthrush (*Formicarius analis*)	+		+	b	e
Sulphur-rumped flycatcher (*Myiobius sulphureipygeus*)				d	e
White-breasted wood-wren (*Henicorhina leucosticta*)		+	+	b	e
Nightingale wren (*Microcerculus marginatus*)			+	b	e
Song wren (*Leucolepis phaeocephalus*)*			+	b	e

* Species disappeared during the 1964–1973 decade. Probably other species disappeared during 1971–1973. a, low density because large for the ecological guild. b, higher densities reached in less mature or dry forests. c, wasp-eating, wanders widely. d, nests over streams, which are uncommon on Barro Colorado. Several other flycatchers that nest over or near streams in second-growth have also been extirpated. e, immigration to Barro Colorado from the mainland unlikely. f, birds not now present on mainland, but could immigrate.

4.4   Island nature reserves

Previously we noted that the ecology of some species is dependent on large areas and that these species will therefore be excluded from some reserves. In general terms there may possibly be two consequences of creating an island reserve in a sea of man-made habitats. The very exclusion of predatory species will in time alter the pattern of species abundance and composition, as also will natural seral changes in the vegetation and changes arising from anthropogenic factors. It is important therefore that reserve managers are aware of these aspects when evaluating areas for nature reserves. A particularly fascinating

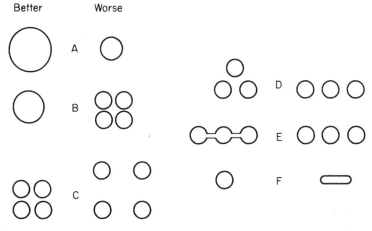

Fig. 4-4   Suggested geometric principles, derived from island biogeographic studies, for the design of nature reserves. (Diamond, J. M. (1975). *Biol. Conserv.*, 7, 129–46.)

illustration of extirpation on Barro Colorado Island (a hilltop of 15.7 km² of lowland tropical forest isolated in 1914 when a lake rose) was provided by WILSON and WILLIS (1975). Of 208 species of birds breeding on the island in the 1920s and 1930s, 45 had gone by 1970, many of which were birds of second growth of forest edge (Table 7). A particularly interesting guild of birds (ecologically related species) were those that fed on the arthropods flushed out by army ants and the larger species in the guild were quickly extirpated. Other losses were thought to fit a pattern of early losses of specialized species.

4.5   Nature reserve design

A further aspect to be considered is the design and structure of the reserve including natural and man-made features: power line rights of way through forests may cause changes in the species composition and distribution of groups of animals such as small mammals and also birds.

Is there an optimum design or mosaic for a nature reserve as island biogeographical theory would suggest (Fig. 4–4)?

This question has to be asked along with other questions. What is the reserve for; to conserve as rich a variety or community of organisms as possible or to conserve a particular group of organisms? When the objectives have been identified then it is important to ask, is there a source of recruitment in or near the reserve and does the reserve have buffet areas to offset the effects of perturbations? Answers to each of these questions requires much research on the organisms' ecology including the dispersal ability of the species. A buffer area might for example be a wet area in which the organisms, (being conserved), do not normally occur. During years when there is an unusually low rainfall, leading to extremely dry conditions elsewhere in the reserve, then the organisms may be able to survive if they can move to areas which will diminish the stress effect caused by the drought. Later the buffer zone would support a population or act as a reservoir for the recruitment of populations to other parts of the reserve. If the objective is to preserve one type of plant community, it would seem wise to incorporate some heterogeneity into the reserve's structure so as to counter the effects of stress caused either by temporary changes in climate or by man's activities.

4.6   Value judgements and objective applications

Several of the criteria previously used in the evaluation of sites for nature reserves have been outlined. There are of course several categories of conservation areas including nature reserves, national parks, resources reserves, and world heritage sites. There is no reason why the mechanisms outlined here for defining priority areas in need of conservation and defining priorities for conservation action, can not be applied to conservation areas such as national parks. The IUCN's Commission on National Parks and Protected areas is developing a system of monitoring to be used for the identification of protected areas in the biogeographical regions. Following completion of the survey or inventory it will be possible to evaluate large areas for national parks and to achieve the objectives related to the evaluation schemes for nature reserves.

Not all the criteria used for evaluation of sites for nature reserves are based on ecological principles but nevertheless it is perhaps more important to ensure that if they are, then the ecological principles should be interpreted correctly. An emphasis on a rigorous scientific approach should be adopted. If such an approach is adopted, perhaps there is then a danger of overlooking the beneficial uses and functions of wildlife. Components which might be considered when evaluating an area for wildlife conservation are shown in Table 8.

A common criticism of the evaluation criteria is that they cannot really be separated and that there is a great deal of overlap. The selection of the criteria is very much a subjective operation and so therefore it is impossible to avoid overlap. Of more importance is the need to be objective in the application and the need to define the objectives of the evaluation.

An example of a rigorous and objective application is seen in an assessment of the ornithological interest of sites listed in the British Trust for Ornithology register of Ornithological Sites. Important and quantitative criteria employed

Table 8 Components increasing wildlife conservation value of an area with their effects on different functions of wildlife indicated by X. (Everett, R. D. (1979). *Biol. Conserv.*, **16**, 207–18.)

Components of wildlife	Agricultural	Medical	Environmental indication	Research	Educational	Aesthetic	Ethical/Moral	Component weighting
1 Richness	X	X	X	X		X	X	6
2 Naturalness	X	X		X	X			4
3 Rarity			X	X			X	3
4 Accessibility				X	X	X		3
5 Previous studies				X	X			2
6 Typicalness				X	X			2
7 Capacity					X			1
8 Species cropped from the wild	X							1
9 Wild relatives of domestic species	X							1
10 Species which function in a similar way to man		X						1
11 Species with known medical uses		X						1
12 Attractive and stimulating species						X		1
13 Species or habitats which contributed to past art works						X		1
14 Species or habitats which contribute to the character of the area						X		1
15 Species which affect the production of a particular crop	X							1
16 Alternate food host sources for agents used in production	X							1

were population size, diversity and rarity. The ornithological interest was classified into three site attributes (population size, species richness, rarity) and the value of each attribute was measured using quantitative criteria in terms of five levels of conservation importance: international, national, regional, county, and local. For example, any site supporting 1% of the biogeographic population of one species could be regarded as internationally important and 1% of a national population could be regarded as nationally important. Scarcer species were placed in one of five classes of national importance and assigned values between one and five. For each site an index of diversity based on the scarce species was obtained by summing values representing the breeding species. Any species with a British population of between 1–1000 pairs was considered to be a

Table 9   The application of evaluation criteria to site data when assessing the ornithological interest of sites for conservation. The example is for a real site of high importance to conservation. (Fuller, R. J. (1980). *Biol. Conserv.*, **17**, 229–39.)

EXAMPLE

A complex of mature flooded gravel workings displaying a wide variety of habitats including extensive willow scrub, alder carr and reedmarsh.

Site data   1 Recorded numbers of species (1968 to 1975): passage 82, breeding 88, wintering 101.
2 Breeding community composition: a—0, b—2, c—6, d—12, e—23.
3 The site supported approximately 20% of the British breeding population of one species.
4 More than 50 pairs of both reed *Acrocephalus scirpaceus* and sedge warblers *A. schoenobaenus* bred.
5 Nesting waterbirds included six species with more than 5 pairs.
6 More than 1000 of both swallows *Hirundo rustica* and sand martins *Riparia riparia* regularly occurred on migration.
7 Two species of wintering wildfowl regularly exceeded 100.
8 Six species of wintering thrushes, finches and buntings regularly exceeded 100.

Assessment   The ornithological features of interest are classified according to their levels of conservation importance.

National   1 The number of breeding species.
2 The quality of the breeding community (index of 73).
3 Rare breeding birds (two class b and six class c).
4 20% of the British breeding population of one species.

Regional   1 The number of wintering species.
2 The *Acrocephalus* breeding populations.

County   1 The number of passage species.
2 The population of nesting waterbirds.
3 Numbers of passage hirundines.
4 Numbers of wintering wildfowl.
5 Numbers of wintering thrushes, finches and buntings.

---

national rarity. The example (Table 9) shows how the criteria are incorporated.

Ecological evaluation has several stages and one further stage should be considered. When evaluating sites for nature reserves it is important to consider the management that may be required for the conservation of the species, habitats and/or communities. There is no doubt at all that some kind of management will be required because, as indicated previously, there will be changes in the ecological characteristics of the reserve. Some of these changes could be detrimental to the aims of establishing the reserve and it is important that we are able to predict at least some of these changes. The evaluation of a potential reserve site therefore requires a statement on the extent and nature ot the management, both for the short term and for the long term. The design of management techniques for nature reserves cannot be considered here but it is a subject well worthy of far more detailed attention.

5 Monitoring and Managing the Environment

Loss of habitats and changes in habitats are not new but the rapid rate of change in some areas is a cause for concern. In general, the greater the rate of change, the greater the conflicts and the greater the need for monitoring and management. Biological indicators have much to offer in the detection of both rates and extent of the changes.

Many county planning departments in Britain are well aware of this loss and change in habitats, and many departments are making use of results from evaluations. What is not clear is the type of evaluation scheme adopted by the planners. There is an obvious need for the provision of ecological information at an early stage in planning. This information should be in the form of an evaluation of the biotic communities but it should also be used to predict the response of the wildlife to different kinds of impact.

Both the scale and amount of detail incorporated in an evaluation will vary according to the circumstances and aims. In general the larger the scale the less detailed the ecological information. This need not be the case, providing it is appreciated that an ecological basis is central to the success of conservation be it at a local level or be it world wide.

5.1 Indicators and monitoring

In Chapter 1 there was an example of a changing environment in the form of the fragmentation of lowland heathlands in southern England. (Fig. 1–3). The extent and the rate of change in this part of England's landscape can be seen in the loss of this particular community. The present fragmented distribution of this heathland is also an indicator of changes in land use but the past and present distribution of these heathlands is indicative of oligotrophic, acid soils. Similarly, the species composition and the floristic diversity of chalk grassland is an indicator of the soil conditions and is also influenced by the climate, aspect, water regime and environmental impacts. The impact of trampling and grazing on chalk grassland and on other communities can easily be seen in the resultant changes in species composition, plant life forms species diversity and relative abundance of the different species. Changes in the species diversity within certain groups of animals such as spiders can also reflect the impact of trampling and on a larger scale, changes in entire river communities can reflect perturbations on the ecosystem.

In river systems there is a natural change from the oligotrophic to the eutrophic state as nutrients accumulate. However, the rate of this change is important and eutrophication resulting from sewage effluents of nitrogenous fertilizers is a well known indication of imbalance in that ecosystem.

Monitoring changes in community species composition, species diversity and relative abundance of species can usefully be employed in measuring the nature and extent of impacts on that community. One advantage is that long term effects can be traced whereas a chemical analysis of soil or water might show only short term effects.

In the same way that communities can act as indicators, some groups of organisms or single species are good indicators. The sensitivity of lichens to air pollutants for example led to the study of their use as indicators and monitors of pollution effects. The most suitable types for this proved to be the foliose forms such as *Hypogymnia physodes* which is widely distributed throughout Europe.

Pollutant accumulation in lichens is comparable with that in higher plants. Some plant species have little or no chance of detoxifying absorbed pollutants due to lack of sufficient pollutant-free times and as a result of accumulating effects in the soil. Interest has been centred around plants as a basis for pollution monitoring. Their suitability rests on the sensitivity of specific plant responses to pollutants in the form of sulphur, fluoride, and chloride.

Some species of animals and plants may be indicators by their absence and some are good indicators because they have narrow tolerances (stenotopic) to physiochemical factors or have a restricted distribution because of narrow habitat requirements (stenoecious). For example the dramatic decline in Britain of the bulbous perennial fritillary (*Fritillaria meleagris*) has been caused mainly by changes in agricultural practices. Characteristic of water meadows, this rare and beautiful species has been affected by the drainage, ploughing and application of artificial fertilizers to riverside meadows.

Another example comes from comparative studies of fish thermal biology which have shown that some species have narrow temperature tolerances. Antarctic fish of the genus *Trematomus* are able to survive in a narrow range of temperatures between $-2.0°C$ and $6°C$ whereas goldfish (*Carassius*) have a very wide temperature tolerance and can survive in temperatures ranging from about $10°$ to $36°C$. Those fish with a wide temperature tolerance could obviously survive large fluctuations in temperature whereas the stenothermal species would be less able to adjust to new temperature conditions. This is an oversimplification but it is true to say that stenotopic species have been used as indicator species because of their narrow tolerances to physiochemical factors.

Construction of life tables and examination of year class or age class frequencies is one approach which can provide information on the response of a population to favourable or unfavourable conditions. Evidence for the decline or complete absence of recruitment to a population may be indicative of a need for management.

Ecological evaluation can therefore take the form of monitoring: a process of repetitive observations of one or more elements or indicators of the environment. An evaluation of the biotic communities on a periodic basis may in some circumstances provide valuable information both at the early stages of planning and in later stages when there has been a change in land use.

5.2 Global monitoring

A world-wide linkage of national and regional environmental monitoring networks was proposed by the Governing Council of the United Nations Environment Plan (UNEP) at Stockholm in 1973. The system is to be called GEMS (Global Environmental Monitoring System) and the plan is to monitor concentrations of priority pollutants such as SO_2, NO_2, the heavy metals and reactive hydrocarbons in the atmosphere, oceans, rivers and lakes, soil and in vegetation and forests. The temporal and geographical spread of the monitoring stations should be appropriate for each pollutant, e.g. daily measurements of water quality indicators, or annual surveys of forest cover. Supplementary data may be collected during natural disasters, high pollution episodes or outbreaks of disease.

5.3 Ecological evaluation and planning

Land is used for all reasons and the demands on land for biological conservation is but one small but integral part of a whole and complex demand. Biological conservation can easily and readily be justified, but it is important to be realistic and consider the demands on the land as a whole. This is where evaluation will have an increasingly important role particularly if the overall objective is to use our resources to the best advantage – hopefully a long term advantage.

A relatively simple and one of the earliest methods for evaluating land for planning purposes was devised by TUBBS and BLACKWOOD (1971). The technique consists of subdividing the area under consideration (basically a map exercise) into 'ecological zones', to each of which is assigned a value, chosen according to criteria from a scale of one to five. The ecological zones are characterised by dominance of one of three broad categories of vegetation related directly to land use: 1, complex of habitats comprising agricultural land; 2, plantation woodland; 3, 'unsown' vegetation. Values for the relative ecological map are shown in Table 10 and an example is shown in Fig. 5–1.

Simple in design, this method has been applied in connection with planning and land use development. It is however only one of a number of techniques which have been tested in Britain in the last ten years. These other techniques fall

Table 10 Criteria and values used in the Tubbs and Blackwood *Relative Ecological Evaluation Map*. (See § 5.3.)

Ecological zone type	Relative Value (I = highest)
Unsown vegetation	I or II: depending on estimate of rarity of habitat type and and scientific importance
Plantation woodland	II or III: with subjective estimate as wildlife reservoir
Agricultural land	II–V: Relative value depends on extent of habitat diversity; assessed on a 4-point scale (0–3) for six features e.g. hedgerows, watercourses, banks and verges.

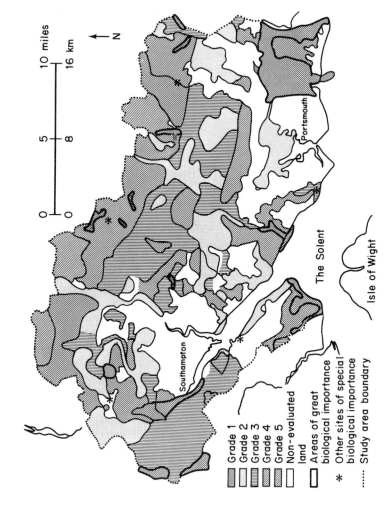

Grade 1

Grade 2

Grade 3

Grade 4

Grade 5

Non-evaluated land

Areas of great biological importance

* Other sites of special biological importance

.... Study area boundary

Southampton

Portsmouth

The Solent

Isle of Wight

N

0   5   10 miles

0   8   16 km

Fig. 5–1 An example of Tubbs and Blackwood's relative ecological evaluation map. (TUBBS and BLACKWOOD (1971). *Biol. Conserv.*, **3**, 169–72).

into two broad categories: those which are different from the Tubbs and Blackwood technique but have a similarly simple approach: those which try to be more objective and necessarily involve the collection of a relatively large amount of data.

Tubbs and Blackwood's method of evaluation has also been modified so that it can be used to assess the ecological damage that is likely to occur by the construction of a new feature such as a road. Development of methods for ecological evaluation of a linear landscape will undoubtedly be of great importance particularly as it is possible to compare alternative plans for development.

5.4 National surveys

Such are the many demands on land in many countries that it seems appropriate to extend ecological evaluation to embrace national landscape surveys. It should be possible, from the results of evaluations, to prepare national scale maps which show the status of the biotic environment along with the results from other evaluations. This kind of approach lends itself to large scale management plans.

In the Netherlands, ecological evaluation of the countryside has been undertaken since about 1968. Many of the Netherland projects are based on fairly intensive aerial photographs which include surveys of plant communities and vegetation complexes, and also inventories of flora, breeding birds and mammals. These biological statements are integrated with results already available from 1:50 000 ground survey maps or those of larger scale, as well as with geomorphical and historical-geographical statements. The majority of maps are on a 1:50 000 scale.

The ecotope concept is the central theme in many investigations and this means that the vegetation-related data are collected on the basis of an ecotopic landscape pattern. Ecotopes are matched to ecotopic complexes, i.e. larger ecological landscape units, also called geotopes. Ecotopes are provisionally differentiated on the grounds of soil characteristics and landscape observations and by means of their identification through vegetation complexities, i.e. comprehensively verified complexes as they relate to plant communities (MAAREL and STUMPEL, 1974). Geotopes likewise are provisionally delineated according to already well-known abiotic features and are verified by means of correlations of vegetation complexes in vegetation orders. Zoological statements are based on these larger units on account of the generally greater activity range of larger animals.

One of the Netherland landscape evaluation projects, the Landelijke Milieu-kartering or Environmental Survey, has resulted in the preparation of an environmental atlas or inventory of the natural environment. The methods for botanical evaluation in this scheme are based mainly on area, species richness and plant community richness. Ecotopes (homogeneous units) form the basis of the evaluation and the total value of the area is the sum of the values attributed to each ecotope thus:

$$\text{total value} = m \sqrt{\frac{\Sigma_{i=1}^{n} = \text{Ap}_i \ W_i^{m}}{\Sigma_{i=1}^{n} = \text{Ap}_i}}$$

where m = general assessment coefficient: if m was 2, the high component value contributes substantially more to the total value than the low component values. If m = ∞ the highest component value would determine the total value

Ap_i = relative surface area of ith ecotope

w_i = value of the ith ecotope on a scale of 0–9

The value of each ecotope is determined by the quality: e.g. presence of nationally rare species, nationally rare plant alliances, and the monument value. Floristic characteristics are in the main examined on the criteria of scarcity (regional, national, international) and diversity and, additionally for plant communities and ecotopes, on the criterion of maturity or irreplaceability.

Evaluation of the fauna in the Environmental Survey of the Netherlands (as yet either poorly developed or non existent in other ecological evaluations) has been undertaken with particular reference to the avian fauna. Rarity and abundance and area are the preferred criteria. Data are aggregated per ecotope or ecochore (comparable heterogeneous units but mostly on the same soil type).

Since 1970 about 65 projects have been either carried out or undertaken in the Netherlands. At planning meetings the results from the surveys are sometimes presented with an interpretation, usually in the form of a scale value: 5 = very valuable (recommended designation, complete protection and optimal natural administration); 4 = valuable (recommended designation, protection sufficient to allow only minor encroachments and to act in close agreement with the nature administration); and so on down to 1 = of scant value, few precautions against encroachments (MAAREL and STUMPEL, 1974).

Expert opinions are presented, where possible with graphics, on the effect, particularly of specific encroachments such as the layout of main streets, town planning, areas of intensive farming, installation of larger sport and recreation projects. Adequate steps for ecological protection are taken and the use of indicator agencies and indicator communities is being developed.

5.5   Environmental impact assessment

In 1969 the International Council of Scientific Unions (ICSU) established the Scientific Committee on Problems of the Environment (SCOPE). This Committee aims to synthesize environmental information on topics such as environmental monitoring and environmental aspects of human settlements. In 1975 the first edition of SCOPE 5 (Environmental Impact Assessment – E.I.A.) was published and this was followed in 1979 by the second edition (MUNN, 1979).

An E.I.A. has been defined as *an activity designed to identify and predict the impact on the biogeophysical environment and on man's health and well-being of legislative proposals, policies, programmes, projects, and operational procedures, and to interpret and communicate information about the impacts* (SCOPE 5: MUNN, 1979).

Many countries have adopted Environmental Impact Assessments; it is mandatory in the United States following the passage in 1970 of the National Environmental Policy Act 1969 (NEPA). The Council on Environmental Quality was created by NEPA to advise the President on environmental matters and generally to oversee compliance by federal agencies. A single piece of legislation (other federal legislation affects actions that are environmentally significant) the purpose is: *to declare a national policy which will encourage productive and enjoyable harmony between man and his environment; to promote efforts which will prevent or eliminate damage to the environment and biosphere and stimulate the health and welfare of man; to enrich the understanding of the ecological systems and natural resources important to the Nation; and to establish a Council on Environmental Quality.*

Canada, Australia and New Zealand have recently introduced legislation which is broadly similar to environmental legislation in America. In western Europe most of the members of the E.E.C. have shown an interest in impact analysis and seem to be in favour of adopting a systematic approach to the assessment of environmental impacts.

In the United Kingdom, considerable interest in E.I.A. has been expressed by a wide variety of groups. Recently there was a meeting to discuss ecological aspects of E.I.A. and this was organized by the Industrial Ecology Group of the British Ecological Society (*Brit. Ecol. Soc. Bull.*, **11**, 1980).

A precedent has been established for E.I.A. in the U.K. This occurred when an environmental impact analysis was commissioned by the consortium developing the Beatrice Field. The voluminous report prepared by SPHERE Environmental Consultants Ltd., published in July 1977, contains a wealth of sociological, biological and economic information and this Environmental Impact Analysis is a major landmark in our progress towards monitoring and managing the environment. Because of the proximity of the field to the coast, an obvious impact to be considered was oil spillage. To this end the Analysis prepared by SPHERE contains suggestions on procedures for clean-up operations and subsequent special monitoring. Of more importance to the natural environment, the Analysis presents detailed results from surveys of the flora and fauna (particularly marine fauna) and also base line information to be used in future monitoring. Apart from the provision of factual information such as species lists, abundance, and distribution, there is little in the way of analysis of the biological data in terms of species diversity. The objectives of the Analysis seem to have been achieved with some success in that given a short period of time SPHERE have provided the much needed and valuable factual information on many aspects of the environment. There is no doubt at all that this kind of analysis will become a necessity as we continue to exploit the resources around us.

Environmental Impact Assessment is in its infancy despite the fact that there are now many E.I.A. methods. In view of the broad range of impacts that should be considered (biogeophysical, social, economic) there seems no doubt that an E.I.A. can not be undertaken by one investigator: a team effort is called for and the team should have representatives from both the natural and social sciences. The broad nature of the E.I.A. does not necessarily mean that each individual aspect is examined in a superficial manner. Specific aspects or impacts could and should be assessed by appropriate experts who then pass on the information to a central team of investigators. The ecologist has a small but integral role in E.I.A. by way of conducting surveys, evaluations and impact assessments. This role could further be broken down into ecological impacts in the aquatic environment or the terrestrial environment. One simple and basic approach could involve a survey of the types and extent of plant communities, habitats and animal species diversity in the area under consideration. Plant indicators in particular would be surveyed (§ 5.1) as also would the status of known protected (§ 2.4) or rare species (§ 4.2.4). The next most logical step would be to consider project effects (the potential impacts) on the habitats and individual species. This requires a specialist knowledge of tolerances of organisms (§ 5.1) to certain kinds of impact and also a specialist knowledge of how project effects would alter ecosystems and communities.

Two of the many schemes are briefly outlined in the next sections. These two have been selected simply because they contrast each other in their overall approach and I leave it to those interested in E.I.A. to consider the role of the ecologist in each of the two schemes.

5.5.1 The Leopold Matrix

There is a variety of methods to assess impacts and one example is that developed by Leopold and others in the United States. It was designed to assess impacts associated with almost any type of construction. The Leopold method is an open-cell matrix containing 100 project actions along the horizontal axis and 88 environmental characteristics and conditions along the vertical axis. The matrix shows 8800 possible interactions, reminding the investigator of the range of effects.

An efficient way of using the matrix seems to be to decide first which actions are likely to occur in the development; usually only 10–20 actions will be important. Each of the actions is then evaluated individually against the existing characteristics of the environment on the vertical axis, and any potentially significant interaction is marked by placing a line diagonally from lower left to upper right across the appropriate grid square. Having marked all the boxes to show possible impacts, the next step is to evaluate the interactions numerically. Within each box representing a significant interaction, a number from 1 to 10 is placed in the upper left-hand corner to indicate the relative magnitude of the impact; 10 represents the greatest magnitude, and 1, the least. In the lower right-hand corner, a number from 1 to 10 is placed representing the relative importance of the impact.

In deciding the value of magnitude for each interaction, the duration of each effect is a major consideration. Some actions may have major short-term impacts which are ameliorated in a few years, and so are of little importance, e.g. oil-drilling rigs which are judged to be noisy and non-aesthetic, but are on location for only short periods of time. Conversely, actions could have little initial impact, but they may produce more significant and persistent secondary

THE LEOPOLD MATRIX

REDUCED GRID SHOWING ALL LIKELY IMPACTS

	EXISTING CONDITIONS OF THE ENVIRONMENT																																		
	PHYSICAL AND CHEMICAL CHARACTERISTICS																FLORA				FAUNA					CULTURAL FACTORS							ECO-LOGY		
	Soils	Landform	Surface water	Underground water	Water quality	Water recharge	Atmospheric quality	Microclimate	Temperature	Floods	Erosion	Deposition	Solution	Compaction and settling	Stability	Air movements	Trees	Shrubs	Microflora	Barriers	Birds	Land animals	Insects	Microfauna	Barriers	Land use-wilderness	Scenic views	Open space qualities	Employment	Population density	Waste disposal	Man-made barriers	Food chains	Brush encroachment	
Modification of habitat	4/2	2/3	2/3		1/2			3/1								2/1	5/4	3/3	3/3	4/2	3/3	3/4	2/1	2/1	3/4	6/6	4/5	5/6					3/4	3/2	63/60
Modification of ground cover	3/2		1/2		1/2			2/1		3/5	3/4	2/4	1/1	3/3	3/4	2/1	5/4	3/3	2/3			4/4	2/1	2/1				6/6					2/3		50/54
Modification of ground-water	3/2		2/3	3/2	3/3	4/3				5/4			2/1		5/4																				27/22
Alteration of drainage	2/3		4/4	4/2	2/2	4/3				4/6		3/2			2/3																				25/25
Burning	3/3						3/1				2/2	1/2					5/6	5/4	4/4		4/5	5/5	3/3	4/3											39/38
Surface changes or paving	2/2	2/4	2/1		3/2									2/3			4/4	3/4	3/3	2/3		4/5	2/2	2/3				5/4							36/40
Noise and vibration							5/2							6/1	6/2						4/2	5/3	4/2	5/2											35/14
Urbanisation	3/2	4/2	3/3	2/1	2/4		4/4	3/2	2/1	3/5	2/3	2/3		1/1	1/2	1/1	4/5	3/4	3/4	2/3	4/5	5/5	3/3	3/3	4/4	5/6	6/6	6/6	4/2	5/4	4/4	3/1			97/99
Roads and trails	2/2	3/2			2/3		3/2	1/1		3/4	2/2	2/2		1/1	2/3	1/1	3/5	3/4	2/3	2/3	4/4	4/5	2/3	2/3	3/5		4/5	5/6	3/2					2/1	61/72
Transmission lines and pipelines		2/1		2/2				1/1						1/1	2/2	1/1											4/5		3/2						16/15
Barriers and fences		1/1						1/1			2/1					1/1						3/4		2/3			5/5	5/4				2/1			22/21
Cut and fill	3/3	4/4	2/3		3/3			2/1		3/3	2/3	2/3		2/2	3/2		3/4	2/3	2/3	2/3		4/5			3/5		3/6	4/6	3/2			2/1			54/65
Landscaping	1/1	4/2	3/2	2/2			1/1	1/1		3/4	2/3	2/3		1/2	2/3	1/1	3/5	2/4	2/4	3/2		5/4	2/2	2/2	4/5	5/6	5/6	4/4	3/3					1/1	64/73
Traffic by automobile					2/4		5/5	3/2									3/5	3/4	2/4		5/5	5/5	3/3	3/3											34/40
Traffic on trails	1/1						2/3										2/4	2/4	1/1		4/4	4/5	1/2	1/2				2/4						2/2	22/32
Spills and leaks	3/4			3/4	3/5					2/4					3/4																				14/21
	30/27	22/19	19/21	16/13	22/30	8/6	23/18	17/11	2/1	26/35	15/18	14/19	3/2	17/14	29/29	9/7	37/46	29/37	24/32	15/16	28/28	51/54	24/22	28/26	17/23	16/18	31/37	42/46	16/11	5/4	4/4	7/3	5/7	8/6	

Fig. 5–2 A condensed grid of the Leopold Matrix for an area of development near Southampton. (These results from an undergraduate Environment Science Student's project (Jennifer Lisk) provide a good illustration of the contents and application of the Leopold Matrix (see § 5.5.1).

effects, and therefore have a major impact in the future: for example water tables could be lowered and have drastic effects on vegetation.

The further stage is to evaluate the numbers in the boxes, and it is usual practice to construct a simplified or reduced matrix consisting only of those actions and environmental characteristics which have been identified as interacting. In some cases, beneficial impacts may be noted, but usually impacts are considered to be detrimental, and any beneficial consequences are included in an accompanying text.

A condensed grid, from the preliminary research carried out by an under-graduate (Jennifer Lisk) on an area in Southampton, shows 228 interactions which are likely to cause environmental impact (Fig. 5–2). This summarises the total number of areas where impact may occur, and also shows the importance and magnitude of these effects. The bottom row on the grid gives the total importance and magnitude of impact on each characteristic of the environment. The column on the side gives the total importance and magnitude of impact due to each action.

The matrix covers both the physical-biological and socio-economic environ-ments, but the list of characteristics is biased towards the physical and biological aspects, with 67 of the 88 items in this field. There is no mechanism for focussing attention on the most critical concerns, and there is no distinction between long- and short-term impacts.

The matrix uses weights to indicate the relative importance and magnitude of effects, but a weakness of the system is that it does not provide explicit criteria for assigning the numerical values to the interactions on the grid (MUNN, 1979). The predictions cannot be synthesized into aggregate indices and the results are only available in the form of a reduced grid which needs a considerable period of time to comprehend the main impacts. The advantage of having all the data in one diagram is in communication of the results of the assessment to interested parties.

There are several other interaction matrices for E.I.A. but most are not as comprehensive as the Leopold Matrix.

5.5.2 McHarg overlays

This approach to impact assessment was suggested by McHarg at the University of Pennsylvania, and in this method a series of overlays is used to identify impacts and show their geographical extent (MUNN, 1979). The use of overlays is well established in planning.

The method is usually applied to very big-scale developments, and the assessor collects information on environmental factors, basically through aerial photo-graphy, with topological and government land inventory maps, field obser-vations, public meetings, and specialist knowledge providing additional data. The areas of concern are grouped into sets of factors, each with a common basis, with no conflicting concerns in one group. A regional map is then drawn for each factor to show its geographical extent and its relative impact in different areas of study. By overlaying the maps to produce a composite impact map the areas of least and greatest impact can be determined visually.

This method of E.I.A. is appropriate for large scale investigations and a typical area for application is of the order of 25 000 km². This area is usually subdivided into convenient geographical units based on uniformly spaced grid points, topographical features or differing land use. The method can be computerized, using unit squares of appropriate size – for the 25 000 km² area unit squares of 500×500 m² are optimal. Information on many variables is obtained for each grid square and grouped into sets of factors. For each factor in each grid square an impact rating is determined on a scale of 1 (low) to 5 (high), with 6 as a special category to indicate an unacceptable impact. The computer produces 'factor maps' with light shading to denote low impact, dark shading denoting high impact, and a different symbol for areas where the impact is unacceptable. A detailed assessment of this method and also the Leopold Matrix can be found in CLARK *et al.* (1978) and MUNN (1979).

5.6 A world strategy

In March 1980, the publication entitled *World Conservation Strategy* was launched in London. This was prepared by the International Union for the Conservation of Nature in collaboration with the United Nations Environment Programme, the World Wildlife fund, the Food and Agriculture Organisation of the United Nations and the United Nations Educational Scientific and Cultural Organization. The aim is to help advance the achievement of sustainable development through the conservation of living resources and the Strategy: (1) explains the contribution of living resource conservation to human survival and to sustainable development; (2) identifies the priority conservation issues and the main requirements for dealing with them; (3) proposes effective ways for achieving the Strategy's aim. The objectives of conservation include maintenance of essential ecological processes and life-support systems and sustainable utilization of species and ecosystems. One of the broad based and ambitious priority requirements deals with genetic diversity: preventions of species extinction, preservation of as many varieties as possible (particularly crop plants and other plants and animals of economic value), preservation of wild forms of economically valuable species, protection of unique ecosystems, and provision of areas for the protection of these ecosystems and biotic communities. There is an emphasis on the need to produce inventories of natural resources as a fundamental basis for the Strategy. This need and the equally valid need to have an ecological basis for conservation emphasizes the importance of ecological evaluation in all its present forms.

6 Conclusions

In a very broad sense, evaluation and conservation might be extended to include several topics: evaluation, reclamation and revegetation of industrial wasteland; conservation of fish populations via models of maximum sustainable yield; watershed management. To include these topics would be illogical because it would detract from an already established and useful relationship between evaluation and conservation. Application of ecology to evaluation and to biological conservation is plausible yet at the same time there is much contention about the lack of ecology in evaluation methods. It might be realistic to replace the term ecological evaluation with nature conservation evaluation because so often we are making value judgements for the purposes of conservation.

There is no doubt that many evaluation methods contain little ecology and that very often there is a mis-interpretation of ecology. This comes as no surprise because the field of ecology, evaluation and conservation is new and has a long way to progress. As biological conservation gathered momentum earlier this century it was inevitable that conservationists would seek a philosophical basis and then later an ecological basis for biological conservation. Determining the conservation priorities of animal and plant species and ascertaining the criteria on which to base selection of sites for nature reserves are two particularly important areas. I suggest that the most important criteria to be used in the evaluation of natural areas and semi-natural areas is habitat diversity.

I am defending a lack of ecology in evaluation by claiming that the subject is new and is still developing. Are there any grounds on which to be optimistic for the future of evaluation and conservation? Although Britain has no national policy for nature conservation it is quite clear that the voluntary organizations have done much to promote successful conservation in Britain. A recent publication from the Society for the Promotion of Nature Conservation confirms this as well as showing that ecology and evaluation is relevant to applied conservation. One of the aims of the SPNC *Nature Reserves Study* was to appraise the existing reserve selection criteria, both scientific and functional, as used by county trusts. I found the conclusions to be particularly gratifying and at the risk of taking material out of context I think it worth noting the following on reserve acquisition criteria in the SPNC *Nature Reserves Study*.

Recognized national status, such as SSSI, is taken into account – the SSSI Schedule usually provides the basis for a site priority list – but local as well as national and regional values play a part in selection.

Qualitative site assessment is based on a selection of the criteria used in the NCR including the presence of rare species. Other criteria such as habitat diversity and size are used, but all trusts assess sites subjectively to some extent.

I conclude that many evaluation methods have been usefully applied, and many are valuable case history studies. There will be much debate about ecology, evaluation and conservation during the next few years but I am confident that this topic has already achieved many of the goals which were once the philosophy of biological conservation.

Appendix: Exercises in Evaluation

When preparing a course of lectures on biological conservation, I could see no better way of introducing the ecological basis of conservation than talking about ecology, evaluation and conservation. The following few and simple exercises have proved relatively successful.

A.1 Conservation and threat numbers

The aim here is to assess the methods used for establishing threat numbers and the objective is to assign a threat number to a small number of species. For the purposes of this practical a high threat number indicates a priority for management and conservation.

A class of students divided into small 'committees' is provided with data sheets. Each data sheet provides information on one species and includes a coloured photograph and also a map of its distribution as recorded from 10 km² (Fig. 2–2). A synopsis of the species' ecology is provided and so also is a brief

Table 11 Suggested criteria for the calculation of a threat number in a practical exercise. (See § 2.2 for additional criteria.)

Criteria	Method of calculation
Rarity	An index of rarity can be obtained from the information provided in an atlas of distribution. Recorded in less than 10 km² score 5 between 11 and 50 10 km² score 4 between 51 and 100 10 km² score 3 between 101 and 400 10 km² score 2 recorded in more than 400 10 km² score 1
Decline	An index of decline can be obtained from information provided in some atlas of distribution. For an 80 per cent decline score 5 appropriate scores follow as above
Dispersal and recruitment	An index of 1 to 5 could again be used and a high score awarded to those species which on information provided seem to have poor powers of dispersal or a low recruitment
Protection	An index of 1 to 5 is used to indicate the degree of protection afforded by the number of protected localities. If the species occurs on no protected sites then it would score 5

Table 12 Example of comparative information provided at the end of a practical exercise.

Species				Threat no.	IUCN	Score/20	Class score
Downy woundwort (*Stachys germanica*)	–	–	–	13	E	20	
*Lady's-slipper (*Cypripedium calceolus*)	–	–	–	12	E	18	
Field eryngo (*Eryngium campestre*)	–	–	–	11	V	17	
*Monkey orchid (*Orchis simia*)	–	–	–	11	V	17	
*Diapensia (*Diapensia lapponica*)	–	–	–	10	V	15	
Early spider-orchid (*Ophrys sphegodes*)	–	–	–	10	V	15	
Purple Spurge (*Euphorbia peplis*)	–	–	–	9	E	14	
Fritillary/snake's head (*Fritillaria meleagris*)	–	–	–	9	V	14	
*Teesdale sandwort (*Minuartia stricta*)	–	–	–	9	V	14	
*Oblong woodsia (*Woodsia ilvensis*)	–	–	–	9	V	14	
*Snowdon lily (*Lloydia serotina*)	–	–	–	8	V	12	
*Drooping saxifrage (*Saxifraga cernua*)	–	–	–	8	V	12	
Breckland speedwell (*Veronica praecox*)	–	–	–	8	E	12	
Hampshire-purslane (*Ludwigia palustris*)	–	–	–	7	R	11	
Alpine catchfly (*Lychnis alpina*)	–	–	–	7	R	11	
*Alpine woodsia (*Woodsia alpina*)	–	–	–	7	R	11	
Tuberous thistle (*Cirsium tuberosum*)	–	–	–	6	R	9	
*Tufted saxifrage (*Saxifraga cespitosa*)	–	–	–	6	R	9	
*Alpine sow-thistle (*Cicerbita alpina*)	–	–	–	5	R	8	
*Mezereon (*Daphne mezereum*)	–	–	–	Considered		1	
Bastard balm (*Melittis melissophylum*)	–	–	–			1	
Monks hood (*Aconitum anglicum (napellus*))	–	–	Not listed		0		
Sea bind-weed (*Calystegia soldanella*)	–	–			0		
Autumn crocus (*Colchicum autumnale*)	–	–			0		
Yellow horned-poppy (*Glaucium flavum*)	–	–	–		0		
Greater broomrate (*Orobanche elatior*)	–	–	–		0		
Grass of Parnassus (*Parnassia palustris*)	–	–	–		0		
Glasswort (*Salicornia europaea*)	–	–	–	–	0		

* Species listed in Schedule 2 of the Conservation of Wild Creatures and Wild Plants Act 1975.

account of any scientific value or economic value. After a preliminary examination of the data sheets each committee selects several criteria (Table 11). On the basis of the information provided for each species, a score is agreed for each of the criteria: the scores are summed to give the threat number. Results for plant species (Table 12) can usefully be compared with published information such as the threat numbers in the *British Red Data Book*.

A.2   Area of nature reserves

Central to this exercise is the construction of a species area curve. If we look at the criteria used for the selection of nature reserves, the aim is often to have as large an area as possible.

Data for this exercise can usefully be based on the information provided in an atlas of the distribution of a group of organisms. There is now a distribution atlas for plants, birds, amphibians and reptiles, non-marine mollusca and bumblebees of the British Isles. The number of species in one 10 km² is first determined by selecting one square and noting each species which has been recorded from that particular square. This area (one 10 km²) is then enlarged to include neighbouring 10 km² and again the total number of species recorded from the larger area is noted. By increasing the area in steps of 10 km² and noting the number of species recorded from each area it is possible to derive a species area curve be it on an over simplified basis (Fig. 4–1). Nevertheless careful examination of the type of curve, the species which are recorded from the larger areas, (see MOORE and HOOPER, 1975) and the broad distribution pattern of each species, provide a useful framework for the discussion. An article in *Nature* (HIGGS and USHER, 1980) takes a fresh look at area of nature reserves and puts forward a good case to show that a number of small reserves have more species than a single large reserve.

A.3   Diversity

If we look at the various methods for evaluation, the criterion of 'diversity' is common to many of the methods. It could be diversity of species, diversity of habitats or diversity of vegetation structure. A useful exercise is to estimate the species diversity (Chapter 4).

Table 13   The chief plant life forms (from Willis, A. J. (1973). *Introduction to Plant Ecology*. George Allen and Unwin Ltd., London).

Phanerophytes	Plants with perennating buds borne well above the ground (trees and shrubs)
Megaphanerophytes and mesophanerophytes	trees more than 8 m in height
Microphanerophytes	trees and shrubs between 2 and 8 m
Nanophanerophytes	shrubs between 0.25 and 2 m
Chamaephytes	Shrubs or herbs with perennating buds raised into the air but not more than 0.25 above ground surface
Hemicryptophytes	Plants with buds formed in the surface of the soil
Geophytes	Plants with perennating buds buried deeply, and on a rhizome, bulb or tuber
Therophytes	Annual plants with a single growing season
Hydrophytes and helophytes	Water plants with perennating buds under the water, and marsh plants with perennating buds in mud below the water level

The Raunkiaer's classification of plant life forms provides one basis for an estimation of structural diversity (Table 13). The characters which have been taken into account in classifying life forms are those which are of ecological importance in adjusting the plant to its habitat.

A simple method for measuring foliage height diversity has been described (MacARTHUR and MacARTHUR, 1961). Where strata can be identified in the vegetation, both the height and density of vegetation in each strata is measured. An estimation of the foliage density can be obtained by moving a board horizontally away from an observer until the board is half obscured by the vegetation. Several estimates would be required for each strata and the foliage height density 'd' would be the reciprocal of the distance between the observer and the board. A profile of the vegetation is obtained by plotting average foliage density against height above the ground. The profile is divided into horizontal layers and 'P'; would be the proportion of the total foliage (area under the foliage profile) of the ith layer.

An index of the foliage height diversity is then given by:

$$- \Sigma_i \, P_i \, \mathrm{Log}_e \, P_i$$

A relationship between birds species diversity and foliage height diversity is shown in Fig. 4–2. Alternative methods for estimation of foliage density could include: a measure of the foliage surface area per m^3; hemi-spherical photographs and an estimate of that fraction of the sky obscured by the foliage.

A.4   Evaluation of natural and semi-natural areas

Field courses provide an opportunity for short term but relatively successful exercises in evaluation of natural or semi-natural areas, based on the methods already outlined. Although sites for environmental education are not abundant in Britain, BOOTH and SINKER (1979) note that some County Trusts, local authorities and the Field Studies Council do provide them. Some nature reserves are also useful because often the biological, ecological and background information is published. There are also published accounts of exercises in evaluation. For example a 'habitat evaluation map' for part of Dorset in England and based on the Tubbs and Blackwood's method of land evaluation (§ 5.3) is contained in the Dorset Naturalist's Trust publication *Wildlife Conservation in the Isle of Purbeck*, 1977.

References

ADAMUS, P. R. and CLOUGH, G. C. (1978). *Biol. Conserv.*, **13**, 165–78.

BOOTH, P. R. and SINKER, C. A. (1979). *J. of Biological Education*, **13**(4), 261–66.

BUNCE, R. G. H. and SHAW, M. W. (1973). *J. Environmental Management*, **1**, 239–58.

CAIRNS, J., ALBAUGH, D. W., BUSEY, F. and CHANEY, D. (1968). *J. Wat. Pollut. Control Fed.*, **40**, 1607–13.

CLARK, B. D., CHAPMAN, K., BISSET, R. and WATHERN, P. (1978). *Built Environment*, **4**, 111–21.

DRURY, W. H. (1974). *Biol. Conserv.*, **6**, 162–9.

ELTON, C. (1966). *The Pattern of Animal Communities*. Chapman and Hall, London.

GEHLBACH, F. R. (1975). *Biol. Conserv.*, **8**, 79–88.

GOLDSMITH, F. B. (1975). *Biol. Conserv.*, **8**, 89–96.

HELLIWELL, D. R. (1973). *J. Environmental Management*, **1**, 85–127.

HIGGS, A. J. and USHER, M. B. (1980). *Nature*, **285**, 568–9.

HOLDGATE, M. W. and WOODMAN, M. J. (1975). *Brit. Ecological Society Bull.*, **6**, 5–14.

INTERNATIONAL UNION FOR THE CONSERVATION OF NATURE. (1975). *Red Data Book. 3. Amphibia and Reptilia.* IUCN Morges, Switzerland.

MAAREL, E. VAN DER and STUMPEL, A. H. P. (1974). *Verh. Ges. Ökol., Erlangen*, 231–40.

MacARTHUR, R. H. and MacARTHUR, J. W. (1961). *Ecology*, **42**, 594–8.

MacARTHUR, R. H. and WILSON, E. O. (1967). *The Theory of Island Biogeography*. Princeton University Press, N.J.

MacFARLAND, G. C., VILLA, J. and TORO, B. (1974). *Biol. Conserv.*, **6**, 118–33.

MOORE, N. W. and HOOPER, M. D. (1975). *Biol. Conserv.*, **8**, 239–50.

MUNN, R. E. (1979). *Environmental Impact Assessment.* (SCOPE 5, second edition). John Wiley & Sons, Chichester & New York.

OXLEY, D. J., FENTON, M. B. and CARMODY, G. R. (1974). *J. appl. Ecol.*, **11**, 51–9.

PERRING, F. H. and FARRELL, L. (1977). *British Red Data Books: 1 Vascular Plants.* SPNC, Lincoln.

PETERKEN, G. F. (1977). *Biol. Conserv.*, **11**, 223–36.

PLOEG, S. W. F. VAN DER and VLIJM, L. (1978). *Biol. Conserv.*, **14**, 197–221.

POLLARD, E., HOOPER, M. D. and MOOR, N. W. (1974). *Hedges.* Collins, London.

RATCLIFFE, D. A. (1977). *A Nature Conservation Review.* Two Vols. Cambridge University Press, Cambridge.

ROUTLEY, R. and ROUTLEY, V. (1974). *The Fight for the Forests*, second edition. Research School of Social Sciences, Australian National University.

SOCIETY FOR THE PROMOTION OF CONSERVATION, (1980). SPNC *Nature Reserves Study.* Compiled by C. Easton and A. E. Smith. SPNC, Lincoln.

TANS, W. (1974). *The Michigan Botanist*, **13**, 31–9.

TUBBS, C. R. and BLACKWOOD, J. W. (1971). *Biol. Conserv.*, **3**, 169–72.

WARD, S. D. and EVANS, D. F. (1976). *Biol. Conserv.*, **9**, 217–33.

WILSON, E. D. and WILLIS, E. O. (1975). *Applied Biogeography.* In, Cody, M. and Diamond, J. M. (1975). *Ecology and Evolution of Communities.* Belknap Press, Harvard.